MongoDB
Interview Questions and Answers

X.Y. Wang

Contents

3   Intermediate   45

5 Expert   113

6 Guru 149

Chapter 1

Introduction

MongoDB has established itself as a prominent NoSQL database solution, offering flexibility, scalability, and performance. As more organizations turn to MongoDB to address their data storage needs, the demand for professionals with MongoDB expertise has grown significantly. "MongoDB: Interview Questions and Answers" has been designed to provide a comprehensive guide for professionals aiming to expand their knowledge of MongoDB and those preparing for job interviews in this domain.

This book is organized into five sections: Basic, Intermediate, Advanced, Expert, and Guru. Each section covers a range of topics, starting with fundamental concepts and progressing to advanced techniques and best practices. The questions and answers are presented in a clear and concise manner, facilitating the reader's understanding of various MongoDB aspects. Throughout the book, real-world scenarios are used to illustrate the practical applications of MongoDB concepts.

Section 1: Basic – This section introduces the foundational concepts of MongoDB, such as the differences between MongoDB and relational databases, BSON, CRUD operations, and indexing. It provides an excellent starting point for those new to MongoDB or looking to brush up on their knowledge.

Section 2: Intermediate – The intermediate section delves deeper into

MongoDB's features and capabilities, such as embedded documents, the aggregation framework, capped collections, and replication. By the end of this section, readers will have gained a solid understanding of MongoDB's core functionality.

Section 3: Advanced – In the advanced section, readers will explore complex topics like transactions, compound indexes, data consistency, and horizontal scaling. This section is ideal for those seeking to gain a deeper understanding of MongoDB's more advanced features and capabilities.

Section 4: Expert – The expert section covers intricate topics like MongoDB consistency models, handling complex data migrations, tuning server settings, and managing hotspots in a sharded cluster. This section is tailored for experienced MongoDB professionals who want to further expand their knowledge and expertise.

Section 5: Guru – The guru section addresses the most advanced and challenging MongoDB concepts, such as schema evolution, global deployments, and field-level encryption. It is targeted at seasoned professionals who want to delve into the most intricate aspects of MongoDB and elevate their mastery to the highest level.

"MongoDB: Interview Questions and Answers" aims to equip readers with the knowledge and confidence required to excel in job interviews and advance their careers in the world of MongoDB. The comprehensive coverage of MongoDB concepts, from basic to guru level, makes this book an invaluable resource for professionals at any stage of their MongoDB journey.

Chapter 2

Basic

2.1 What is MongoDB, and why would you choose it over a relational database?

MongoDB is a popular NoSQL database management system that is used to store, manage, and retrieve unstructured data. It is a document-oriented database that stores data in flexible, schema-less JSON-like documents, where each document represents a single record in the database. MongoDB is designed to scale effortlessly, making it an excellent choice for storing large amounts of data across distributed systems.

Some reasons why you might choose MongoDB over a relational database include:

1. Flexibility: Traditional relational databases typically have a strict schema, which means that the data that can be stored in a table is strictly defined by the table's schema. However, MongoDB is schema-less and can store any kind of data, which makes it a more versatile option.

2. Performance: MongoDB is designed to be highly performant, even when working with large datasets. This is because it uses a number of features like sharding, indexing, and query optimization to ensure

that data retrieval is fast and efficient.

3. Scalability: MongoDB is highly scalable and can handle large volumes of data without sacrificing performance. This is because it is designed to work in distributed environments and can be easily scaled horizontally by adding more nodes to a cluster.

4. Cost: MongoDB is open-source, which means that it is free to use and can be easily customized to suit your specific needs. This makes it a more cost-effective option than traditional relational databases, which can be expensive to license and maintain.

Here is some sample code to illustrate how simple it is to work with MongoDB in Python:

```python
import pymongo

# Connect to MongoDB
client = pymongo.MongoClient("mongodb://localhost:27017/")

# Create a database
db = client["mydatabase"]

# Create a collection
col = db["customers"]

# Insert a document
mydict = { "name": "John", "address": "Highway␣37" }
x = col.insert_one(mydict)

# Print the newly added document ID
print(x.inserted_id)
```

In this code, we first connect to a MongoDB instance running on localhost. We then create a database and a collection within that database. Next, we insert a new document into the collection, specifying the document's fields as a Python dictionary. Finally, we print the ID of the newly added document to the console.

2.2 Explain the basic components of a MongoDB document and how it differs from a traditional SQL table.

In MongoDB, the basic unit of data storage is a document. A document is a set of key-value pairs, similar to a JSON object, where the keys are strings, and the values can be of many types including other documents, arrays, strings, integers, and floating-point numbers. A document can have dynamic schema, meaning that different documents within the same collection can have different sets of fields.

On the other hand, in traditional SQL databases, the basic unit of data storage is a table. A table is made up of columns, each with its own data type, and rows, each representing a single record. Tables have a fixed schema, meaning that every row in a table has the same set of columns.

The main differences between a MongoDB document and a traditional SQL table are:

1. Dynamic vs Static Schema: MongoDB documents have dynamic schema, meaning that each document can have a different set of fields. For example, a document representing a person may have fields for name, address, and phone number, while another document representing a company may have fields for name, address, website, and number of employees. In a traditional SQL table, the schema is static, meaning that each row has the same set of columns.

2. Nested Data: In MongoDB, documents can contain nested data, meaning that a document can have fields that themselves contain documents or arrays of documents. This allows for more complex and hierarchical data structures than are possible with traditional SQL tables.

3. No Joins: MongoDB does not use joins, which are a common feature of SQL databases. Instead, MongoDB encourages denormalization, which means that related data is often stored together in a single document rather than split across multiple tables as it might be in a SQL database.

4. Scale-out Architecture: MongoDB is designed to be distributed and scalable, while traditional SQL databases were originally designed for single-server environments. MongoDB can automatically shard collections across multiple servers, allowing for horizontal scaling as data volumes increase.

Overall, MongoDB's document-oriented data model provides more flexibility and scalability than traditional SQL databases, at the cost of some of the powerful querying capabilities that SQL databases provide.

2.3   What is BSON, and how is it related to JSON?

BSON is a binary representation of JSON data. It stands for Binary JSON. BSON was created to overcome some limitations of JSON, such as the lack of support for certain data types, like dates, and inefficient storage and parsing of JSON data. BSON is a binary-encoded serialization of JSON, which makes it more compact and efficient than JSON.

BSON and JSON are related in the sense that they share the same data model and syntax for representing data. BSON can be seen as an extension of JSON that adds additional data types and optimizations for binary storage and transmission.

BSON allows for more efficient and faster transmission of data between client and server, especially over a network, since it is more compact than JSON. BSON stores data in a binary format, which makes it more efficient to transmit and parse, as it can be read and written directly from memory.

Here is an example of how JSON data is represented in BSON:

JSON representation:

```
{
    "name": "John",
    "age": 30,
    "location": {
        "city": "New York",
        "state": "NY"
    }
}
```

BSON representation:

```
\\x32\\x00\\x00\\x00         // total document size
\\x02                        // element type 0x02 = String
name\\x00                    // field name
\\x04\\x00\\x00\\x00John\\x00 // field value
\\x10\\x00\\x00\\x00\\x0f     // element type 0x10 = Int32
age\\x00                     // field name
\\x1e\\x00\\x00\\x00          // field value
\\x03                        // element type 0x03 = Object
location\\x00                // field name
\\x26\\x00\\x00\\x00          // total size of location object
\\x02                        // element type 0x02 = String
city\\x00                    // field name
\\x0b\\x00\\x00\\x00New York\\x00 // field value
```

```
\\x02                        // element type 0x02 = String
state\\x00                   // field name
\\x02\\x00\\x00\\x00NY\\x00   // field value
\\x00                        // end of document
```

As you can see, BSON has added additional information that is not present in the original JSON representation in order to make it more efficient when transmitting and storing data.

2.4   Describe the differences between a MongoDB collection and a relational database table.

A MongoDB collection is a grouping of MongoDB documents that have no formal relationships; it can be thought of as the equivalent of a table in a relational database. However, there are several differences between a MongoDB collection and a relational database table, which I will outline below:

1. Schema: In a relational database, each table has a well-defined schema that defines the columns and their data types. Data in a table must adhere to this schema. In contrast, MongoDB collections do not follow a strict schema, which allows for greater flexibility in managing data. Documents within a collection can have different fields or different types for the same field.

2. Relationships: In a relational database, tables can be related to each other through foreign keys. MongoDB, on the other hand, employs a denormalized data model where related data is nested within a document, rather than being stored in separate tables. References and relationships can still be formed but they are not enforced by the database.

3. Querying: In a relational database, SQL is used to query data. In MongoDB, queries are written in JSON-like syntax that is easy to understand.

4. Scalability: Relational databases are typically vertically scalable, where you increase the resources of the server (such as adding more RAM or a faster CPU) to improve performance. MongoDB, on the

other hand, is horizontally scalable, where you can add more nodes to a cluster to improve performance.

An example of a document in a MongoDB collection:

```
{
  "_id" : ObjectId("5ec4058c1c90750c7643d3e4"),
  "name": "John Doe",
  "age": 32,
  "address": {
    "street": "123 Main St",
    "city": "Anytown",
    "state": "CA",
    "zip": "12345"
  },
  "interests": ["hiking", "reading", "traveling"]
}
```

In this example, there is no strict schema, and the document contains nested data and an array. In contrast, the equivalent relational database table would have defined columns with strict data types.

2.5   What is the role of the _id field in a MongoDB document, and how is it generated?

In MongoDB, the _id field is a unique identifier assigned to each document in a collection. It serves as the primary key for the document, and is required for all documents.

The _id field can be assigned manually by the user, or it can be automatically generated by MongoDB. If the user does not provide a value for _id when inserting a document, MongoDB will create a unique ObjectId and assign it to the document as the _id field.

An ObjectId is a 12-byte value consisting of a time stamp, a machine identifier, a process id, and a counter. This provides a high degree of uniqueness even across distributed systems, making it a reliable choice for generating _id values.

Here's an example of inserting a document into a MongoDB collection with a manually-assigned _id field:

```
db.users.insertOne({_id: "john_doe", name: "John Doe", age: 42})
```

And here's an example of inserting a document with an automatically-generated ObjectId:

```
db.users.insertOne({name: "Jane␣Smith", age: 35})
```

In the second example, MongoDB will generate an ObjectId for the _id field of the document.

2.6   How do you create a database and a collection in MongoDB?

To create a database and a collection in MongoDB, you need to follow the following steps:

1. Start by opening up the MongoDB shell by running the command 'mongo' in your terminal. This will launch the MongoDB shell and connect to the default 'test' database.

2. To create a new database, you can use the 'use' command followed by the name of the new database you want to create. For example, to create a new database called 'mydb', run the following command:

```
use mydb
```

Note that this command will not create the database until you create a collection.

3. To create a collection, you can use the 'db.createCollection()' method. For example, to create a new collection called 'mycollection' in the 'mydb' database, run the following command:

```
db.createCollection("mycollection")
```

By default, MongoDB does not enforce any schema on the collections that it creates. However, you can add constraints on the fields of the documents using validators or indexes.

Here is an example that shows how to create a collection with validators applied to its fields:

```
db.runCommand({
```

```
create: "students",
validator: {
  $jsonSchema: {
    bsonType: "object",
    required: [ "name", "age", "courses" ],
    properties: {
      name: {
        bsonType: "string",
        description: "must␣be␣a␣string␣and␣is␣required"
      },
      age: {
        bsonType: "int",
        minimum: 18,
        maximum: 30,
        description: "must␣be␣an␣integer␣in␣the␣range␣18-30"
      },
      courses: {
        bsonType: "array",
        items: {
          bsonType: "string",
          description: "must␣be␣a␣string"
        }
      }
    }
  }
}
})
```

This 'db.runCommand()' example creates the 'students' collection with the following validators on its fields:

- 'name': must be a string and is required.

- 'age': must be an integer in the range 18-30.

- 'courses': must be an array of strings.

By applying validators like this, we can ensure that the data stored in MongoDB is consistent and can also help prevent malicious attacks that may try to inject data that violates the schema constraints.

2.7   Explain the concept of a schema-less design in MongoDB, and how does it impact database operations?

The schema-less design is one of the core features of MongoDB, which is a NoSQL document-oriented database. In a traditional RDBMS (Relational Database Management System), a schema is a blueprint that defines the structure of the data stored in the database, including the tables, fields, data types, and relationships between the tables.

In contrast, MongoDB does not enforce any predefined schema design. Instead, the data is stored in flexible JSON-like documents, where each document can have a different structure, including different fields, data types, and nesting levels, within the same collection. This allows developers to store and query data without having to worry about the complexity of upfront schema design, leaving the flexibility to update the schema and adapt to changing requirements over time in a cost-effective manner, without downtime or performance impact.

The flexibility of a schema-less design benefits developers in several ways. Firstly, it reduces complexity and accelerates development by eliminating the need for upfront schema design and data migration. Secondly, it supports dynamic data with different structures, making it more resilient to changes in data requirements, especially in complex and rapidly changing applications. Thirdly, it maximizes the developer productivity, as it enables them to work with data in a much more agile and iterative way.

However, this also has some impacts on database operations. Since there is no schema enforcement, it means that data validation becomes the responsibility of the application developer rather than the database. Also, since the schema-less design can lead to data redundancy and unnecessary duplication, it may increase the storage requirements and affect the performance of the database when dealing with large datasets.

Nevertheless, MongoDB provides various ways to manage schema design through indexes, validations, and aggregation. For example, indexes are used to optimize query performance for frequently searched fields; validation rules can be applied to enforce certain data constraints such as data type, value range or required fields; and aggregation pipelines can be utilized to combine and manipulate data from different collections or documents.

In conclusion, a schema-less design in MongoDB provides significant benefits to application developers in terms of flexibility, agility, and cost-effectiveness, but it comes at a cost of additional responsibility for data validation and possible performance and storage concerns.

2.8   What is the role of indexing in Mon-goDB, and how does it improve query performance?

In MongoDB, indexing plays a critical role in improving the perfor-mance of queries. An index is a data structure that organizes data in a way that enables faster data access. When an index exists on a collection, MongoDB can use it to quickly locate documents within that collection.

When performing a query in MongoDB, the database engine examines the query predicates and then attempts to find the documents that match those predicates. If an index exists on the collection being queried, MongoDB can use it to reduce the number of documents it needs to examine to satisfy the query. This makes the query more efficient, as fewer documents need to be scanned.

Indexes are created on documents in MongoDB based on the values contained in specific fields. These indexes can be thought of as a key-value store, where the key is the indexed field value, and the value is a pointer to the document that contains that value. When a query is executed that references the indexed field, the MongoDB engine can use the index to quickly locate the documents that match the search criteria.

Let's say we have a collection called "users" that contains a document for each user, with each document having the following fields:

_id - The unique identifier for the user.

username - The username of the user.

email - The email address of the user.

If we frequently need to search for users by their email address, we can create an index on the **email** field to improve query performance. We can create the index using the following command:

```
db.users.createIndex({ email: 1 })
```

This creates a new index on the **email** field. The **1** indicates that the index should be in ascending order.

Now, if we run a query to find all users with the email address
"john@example.com", MongoDB can use the index to quickly locate
the documents that match this criteria. The query might look like
this:

```
db.users.find({ email: 'john@example.com' })
```

If we didn't have an index on the `email` field, MongoDB would have to
scan through every document in the collection to find matches for our
query. With the index, it can quickly locate documents that match
the search criteria, which can greatly improve query performance.

In summary, indexing plays a critical role in improving query performance in MongoDB. When an index exists on a collection, MongoDB
can use it to quickly locate documents that match search criteria,
reducing the amount of time and resources needed to satisfy a query.

2.9   How do you perform basic CRUD (Create, Read, Update, and Delete) operations in MongoDB?

MongoDB is a document-oriented NoSQL database that provides a
flexible and scalable data model. It uses BSON(Binary JSON) format
to store data.

The CRUD operations in MongoDB are performed using the following
methods:

1) Create Operation:

To create a new document in MongoDB, the 'insertOne()' or 'insert-
Many()' method is used. The syntax is as follows:

```
db.collection.insertOne(document)
db.collection.insertMany(documents)
```

Here, 'db.collection' refers to the name of the collection in which the
document(s) will be inserted. The 'document' parameter is a JSON
object that represents the data to be inserted.

Example:

```
//Insert a single document
db.users.insertOne({name: "John Doe", age: 30})

//Insert multiple documents
db.users.insertMany([
  {name: "Bob Smith", age: 25},
  {name: "Jane Doe", age: 27},
  {name: "Alice Johnson", age: 23}
])
```

2) Read Operation:

To read data from a MongoDB collection, the 'find()' method is used. The syntax is as follows:

```
db.collection.find(query, projection)
```

Here, 'query' is an optional parameter that specifies the conditions for selecting documents. The 'projection' parameter is also optional and is used to specify the fields to be returned in the result.

Example:

```
//Find all documents in a collection
db.users.find()

//Find documents that match a condition
db.users.find({age: {$gt: 25}})

//Find documents and return only selected fields
db.users.find({}, {name: 1, age: 1})
```

3) Update Operation:

To update data in MongoDB, the 'updateOne()' or 'updateMany()' method is used. The syntax is as follows:

```
db.collection.updateOne(filter, update, options)
db.collection.updateMany(filter, update, options)
```

Here, 'filter' specifies the condition for selecting the documents to be updated. The 'update' parameter is a JSON object that specifies the modifications to be made.

Example:

```
//Update a single document
db.users.updateOne({name: "John Doe"}, {$set: {age: 31}})
```

```
//Update multiple documents
db.users.updateMany({age: {$lt: 25}}, {$inc: {age: 1}})
```

4) Delete Operation:

To delete data in MongoDB, the 'deleteOne()' or 'deleteMany()' method is used. The syntax is as follows:

```
db.collection.deleteOne(filter)
db.collection.deleteMany(filter)
```

Here, 'filter' specifies the condition for selecting the documents to be deleted.

Example:

```
//Delete a single document
db.users.deleteOne({name: "John Doe"})

//Delete multiple documents
db.users.deleteMany({age: {$lt: 25}})
```

In conclusion, MongoDB provides a simple but powerful set of functions to perform basic CRUD operations. These functions can be chained together to perform complex queries on the document-oriented data model.

2.10   What are MongoDB query operators, and can you provide a few examples?

In MongoDB, there are special query operators that allow for more specific and complex queries to be performed on collections. These operators are preceded by a dollar sign ($), and they can be used with query matchers to refine the results of a query. Here are some examples of MongoDB query operators:

1. $eq - matches documents where the value of a field equals a specified value.

Example: Find all documents where the name field equals "John".

"' db.collection.find(name: $eq: "John") "'

2. $ne - matches documents where the value of a field does not equal a specified value.

Example: Find all documents where the name field is not equal to "John".

"' db.collection.find(name:$ne: "John") "'

3. $gt/$gte - matches documents where the value of a field is greater than or greater than or equal to a specified value.

Example: Find all documents where the age field is greater than 30.

"' db.collection.find(age:$gt: 30) "'

4. $lt/$lte - matches documents where the value of a field is less than or less than or equal to a specified value.

Example: Find all documents where the age field is less than or equal to 30.

"' db.collection.find(age:$lte: 30) "'

5. $in - matches documents where the value of a field matches any value in a specified array.

Example: Find all documents where the name field is either "John" or "Jane".

"' db.collection.find(name:$in: ["John", "Jane"]) "'

6. $nin - matches documents where the value of a field does not match any value in a specified array.

Example: Find all documents where the name field is neither "John" nor "Jane".

"' db.collection.find(name:$nin: ["John", "Jane"]) "'

These are just a few examples of the MongoDB query operators available. There are many other operators that can be used to create more complex queries.

2.11   How can you project specific fields while querying data in MongoDB?

In MongoDB, we can use the 'project' method to specify which fields to retrieve while querying data.

Consider a MongoDB collection 'students' with the following documents:

```
{
    "_id" : ObjectId("614b0e3e3fe1e7bf473990bc"),
    "name" : "Alice",
    "age" : 22,
    "gender" : "female",
    "course" : "mathematics"
}
{
    "_id" : ObjectId("614b0e513fe1e7bf473990bd"),
    "name" : "Bob",
    "age" : 20,
    "gender" : "male",
    "course" : "history"
}
```

To query for documents with specific fields projected, we can use the 'project' method. For example, to retrieve only the 'name' field:

```
db.students.find({}, {name: 1})
```

This will return the following result:

```
{ "_id" : ObjectId("614b0e3e3fe1e7bf473990bc"), "name" : "Alice" }
{ "_id" : ObjectId("614b0e513fe1e7bf473990bd"), "name" : "Bob" }
```

In the second argument of the 'find' method, we specify which fields to include ('name' in this case) and set the value to '1' to tell MongoDB to include the field. If we wanted to exclude a field, we could set the value to '0'.

We can also project multiple fields using the same syntax. For example:

```
db.students.find({}, {name: 1, age: 1})
```

This will return the following result:

```
{ "_id" : ObjectId("614b0e3e3fe1e7bf473990bc"), "name" : "Alice", "age" : 22
    }
{ "_id" : ObjectId("614b0e513fe1e7bf473990bd"), "name" : "Bob", "age" : 20 }
```

Note that we can also use the '_id' field to project or exclude. By default, MongoDB includes the '_id' field in all query results. To exclude the '_id' field, we can set its value to '0'. For example:

```
db.students.find({}, {name: 1, age: 1, _id: 0})
```

This will return the following result:

```
{ "name" : "Alice", "age" : 22 }
{ "name" : "Bob", "age" : 20 }
```

2.12   What is the difference between the findOne() and find() methods in MongoDB?

In MongoDB, 'findOne()' and 'find()' are both methods available for querying database collections but they have different use cases and return different results.

'findOne()' returns one document that matches the query criteria while 'find()' returns a cursor that can be used to iterate over all the documents that match the query criteria.

Here is a more detailed explanation of each method:

findOne()

The 'findOne()' method returns the first document that matches the query criteria. If there are multiple matching documents, it will only return the first one in natural order. The general syntax of 'findOne()' method is as follows:

```
db.collection.findOne(query, projection)
```

where 'query' specifies the search criteria and 'projection' specifies the fields to be returned. The 'projection' parameter is optional and can be omitted.

Example:

Let's say we have a 'users' collection with the following documents:

```
{ "_id" : ObjectId("60d59df73a194d1f78e27720"), "name" : "John", "age" : 30 }
{ "_id" : ObjectId("60d59e413a194d1f78e27721"), "name" : "Jane", "age" : 25 }
{ "_id" : ObjectId("60d59e4c3a194d1f78e27722"), "name" : "Bob", "age" : 35 }
```

If we run the following code:

```
db.users.findOne({name: "John"})
```

It will return the following result:

```
{ "_id" : ObjectId("60d59df73a194d1f78e27720"), "name" : "John", "age" : 30 }
```

find()

The 'find()' method returns all documents that match the query criteria. The general syntax of 'find()' method is as follows:

```
db.collection.find(query, projection)
```

where 'query' specifies the search criteria and 'projection' specifies the fields to be returned. The 'projection' parameter is optional and can be omitted.

Example:

Using the same 'users' collection, if we run the following code:

```
db.users.find({age: {$gt: 25}})
```

It will return the following result:

```
{ "_id" : ObjectId("60d59df73a194d1f78e27720"), "name" : "John", "age" : 30 }
{ "_id" : ObjectId("60d59e4c3a194d1f78e27722"), "name" : "Bob", "age" : 35 }
```

Note that this returned all documents that have their age greater than 25.

In conclusion, 'findOne()' returns a single document while 'find()' returns a cursor that can be used to iterate over multiple documents. Use 'findOne()' when you only need to access a single document and use 'find()' when you need to access multiple documents.

2.13 How do you sort and limit the results of a query in MongoDB?

Sorting and limiting the results of a query are common operations in MongoDB, and they are achieved by using the 'sort' and 'limit' methods respectively.

To sort the results of a query, you can use the 'sort' method to specify one or more fields to sort by, and the sort order for each field (either ascending or descending). For example, to sort a collection of products by their prices in descending order, you can use the following query:

```
db.products.find().sort({ price: -1 })
```

This query sorts the results of the 'find()' method by the 'price' field in descending order (-1).

To limit the number of results returned by a query, you can use the 'limit' method to specify the maximum number of documents to return. For example, to limit the number of documents returned by the previous query to 10, you can use the following query:

```
db.products.find().sort({ price: -1 }).limit(10)
```

This query returns the first 10 documents sorted by the 'price' field in descending order.

It is also possible to combine the 'sort' and 'limit' methods in a single query to retrieve a sorted and limited subset of documents. For example, to retrieve the 10 most expensive products in the collection, you can use the following query:

```
db.products.find().sort({ price: -1 }).limit(10)
```

This query sorts the documents by their 'price' field in descending order and returns the first 10 documents in the sorted list.

It is important to note that the 'sort' and 'limit' methods should be used in conjunction with an appropriate index to avoid querying the entire collection and causing performance issues. For example, to optimize the query above, you could create an index on the 'price' field.

2.14   What is the MongoDB aggregation framework, and why is it useful?

The MongoDB aggregation framework is a powerful tool used for processing and transforming data within collections. It allows users to perform complex data processing operations on large sets of data in a fast and efficient manner.

Aggregation in MongoDB refers to data processing operations such as grouping, filtering, and sorting that allow a user to extract meaningful insights from the data stored in a collection. Some of the key features of the MongoDB aggregation framework include:

1. Pipeline-based processing: The aggregation framework is a pipeline-based processing system. This means that data processing operations can be linked together as a series of steps, with the output of each step serving as the input to the next.

2. Fast and efficient: The aggregation framework is designed to be fast and efficient. It takes full advantage of MongoDB's indexing capabilities and other performance optimizations to process large datasets quickly and with minimal overhead.

3. Rich set of operators: MongoDB provides a rich set of operators that can be used in aggregation pipelines. These include operators for grouping, filtering, sorting, transforming, and projecting data.

4. Flexible output formats: The aggregation framework allows users to customize the format of the output data. This includes the ability to group data, calculate summaries, and create custom fields.

5. Scalability: The MongoDB aggregation framework is scalable, allowing it to handle large volumes of data across multiple servers.

The aggregation framework is particularly useful for business intelligence applications where large datasets need to be processed and transformed into meaningful insights. It can also be used for reporting and analytics, allowing users to gain a deeper understanding of the data stored in their collections.

Here's an example of how the aggregation framework can be used to group and count the number of documents in a collection by a specific key:

```
db.products.aggregate([
  { $group: { _id: "$category", count: { $sum: 1 } } }
])
```

This aggregation pipeline groups the documents in the "products" collection by their "category" field and counts the number of documents in each group. The output will be a list of objects, with each object containing the "_id" field (which is the value of the "category" field) and the "count" field (which is the number of documents in that group).

2.15   How do you update a document in MongoDB, and what are some common update operators?

To update a document in MongoDB, we can use the 'updateOne' or 'updateMany' method, depending on whether we want to update a single document or multiple documents in a collection. The general syntax of the 'updateOne' method is as follows:

```
db.collection.updateOne(
  <filter>,
  <update>,
  {
    upsert: <boolean>,
    writeConcern: <document>,
    collation: <document>,
    arrayFilters: [ <filterdocument1>, ... ],
    hint: <document|string>    // Available starting in MongoDB 4.2.1
  }
)
```

where:

- '<filter>' is a document that matches the filter for the document or documents to update.

- '<update>' is a document containing update operators and their corresponding values.

Some common update operators in MongoDB are:

1. '$set': Sets the value of a field in a document. For example, to set the value of the field 'score' to 90 in a document that matches a certain filter, we can use the following update operation:

```
db.collection.updateOne(
  { name: "John" },
  { $set: { score: 90 } }
)
```

2. '$unset': Removes a field from a document. For example, to remove the 'score' field from a document that matches a certain filter, we can use the following update operation:

```
db.collection.updateOne(
  { name: "John" },
  { $unset: { score: "" } }
)
```

3. '$inc': Increments the value of a field by a specified amount. For example, to increment the value of the 'score' field by 10 in a document that matches a certain filter, we can use the following update operation:

```
db.collection.updateOne(
  { name: "John" },
  { $inc: { score: 10 } }
)
```

4. '$push': Adds an element to an array field. For example, to add the element '"history"' to the 'subjects' array field in a document that matches a certain filter, we can use the following update operation:

```
db.collection.updateOne(
  { name: "John" },
  { $push: { subjects: "history" } }
)
```

5. '$pull': Removes all occurrences of an element from an array field. For example, to remove all occurrences of the element '"math"' from the 'subjects' array field in a document that matches a certain filter, we can use the following update operation:

```
db.collection.updateOne(
  { name: "John" },
  { $pull: { subjects: "math" } }
)
```

These are just some of the commonly used update operators in MongoDB. There are many more operators available, and they provide a
powerful way to manipulate and update documents in our collections.

2.16   Explain the concept of upsert in Mon-
          goDB, and how can it be used?

In MongoDB, upsert is a feature that allows you to update a document
if it exists or insert a new document if it doesn't exist. The term
"upsert" is a combination of the words "update" and "insert". This
feature is particularly useful when you are working with data that
may or may not already exist in your database, and you don't know
whether you need to perform an update or an insert.

The syntax for an upsert operation in MongoDB is as follows:

```
db.collection.update(
   <query>,
   <update>,
   {
     upsert: <boolean>,
     ...
   }
)
```

The '<query>' parameter specifies the document or documents that
you want to update or insert. If the document already exists in the
collection, the '<update>' parameter specifies how you want to modify the existing document, similar to a regular 'update()' operation.
If the document does not exist in the collection, the '<update>' parameter specifies the document to be inserted.

The 'upsert' option is what makes this operation an upsert. If it is
set to 'true', MongoDB will insert the document specified in '<up-
date>' if no documents match the '<query>' parameter. If it is set
to 'false' (the default), MongoDB will not insert a new document if
no documents match the '<query>' parameter.

Here is an example of how to use an upsert operation in MongoDB.
First, let's assume that we have a collection called 'users', which stores
documents representing user accounts. Each document has an '_id'
field, which is a unique identifier for the user account. If the user

account corresponding to a given '_id' already exists in the collection, we want to update it with new information. If the user account does not exist, we want to create a new one with the given '_id':

```
// Update or create a user account with the given _id
const userId = '123';

db.users.update(
  { _id: userId },
  { $set: { email: 'john@example.com', name: 'John' } },
  { upsert: true }
);
```

In this example, we are updating or creating a user account with the '_id' '123'. The 'email' and 'name' fields are set to new values. If a user account with the '_id' '123' already exists in the 'users' collection, its 'email' and 'name' fields will be updated with the new values. If no user account with the '_id' '123' exists in the collection, a new document will be inserted with the given '_id', 'email', and 'name' fields.

2.17   How do you delete a document or an entire collection in MongoDB?

To delete a document or an entire collection in MongoDB, you can use the 'deleteOne()', 'deleteMany()', or 'drop()' method.

The 'deleteOne()' method is used to delete a single document that matches a specified filter. For example, to delete a document with a specific '_id' field value, you can use the following code:

```
db.collection.deleteOne({ _id: ObjectId("document_id_here") })
```

The 'deleteMany()' method is used to delete multiple documents that match a specified filter. For example, to delete all documents where the 'status' field is set to 'inactive', you can use the following code:

```
db.collection.deleteMany({ status: "inactive" })
```

The 'drop()' method is used to delete an entire collection. For example, to delete a collection named 'myCollection', you can use the following code:

```
db.myCollection.drop()
```

It is important to note that these methods will permanently delete the specified documents or collections, so it is recommended to use them with caution. You should always double-check that you are deleting the correct data before performing these operations.

2.18   What is replication in MongoDB, and why is it important?

In MongoDB, replication refers to the process of synchronizing data across multiple database servers. Replication involves copying the data from a primary server to one or more secondary servers. The primary server is responsible for processing write operations, while the secondary servers are responsible for read operations.

Replication is an essential feature of MongoDB as it provides high availability and fault tolerance for your database. By replicating your data across multiple servers, you can ensure that your database remains available even in case of a server failure. If the primary server fails, one of the secondary servers can be automatically promoted to become the new primary server, ensuring that write operations can continue uninterrupted.

Replication also improves read performance by allowing you to distribute read operations across multiple servers. This can help to reduce the load on the primary server and improve overall system performance.

In MongoDB, replication is implemented using replica sets. A replica set is a group of MongoDB servers that together maintain the same data set. One server is designated as the primary server, while the others are secondary servers. The primary server receives all write operations, and these operations are then replicated to the secondary servers. The replica set also includes an arbiter, which is responsible for resolving conflicts if multiple servers attempt to become the primary server at the same time.

In order to set up replication in MongoDB, you first need to create

a replica set by initializing each server with the same configuration
file. You can then add each server to the replica set using the rs.add()
command.

Here is an example of setting up a replica set in MongoDB:

```
rs.initiate()
rs.add("mongo-2.example.com:27017")
rs.add("mongo-3.example.com:27017")
```

In this example, we first initialize the replica set using the rs.initiate()
command. We then add two secondary servers to the replica set using
the rs.add() command.

Overall, replication is a critical feature of MongoDB that provides
high availability and fault tolerance for your database. By replicating
your data across multiple servers, you can ensure that your database
remains available even in the case of a server failure.

2.19   What is sharding in MongoDB, and how does it help with scalability?

Sharding, in the context of MongoDB, is the way of horizontally
scaling data across multiple servers or nodes. It is a technique that
distributes data across multiple machines and enables MongoDB to
support large-scale data needs with increased performance and scalability.

In sharding, a large dataset is partitioned into multiple smaller chunks,
called shards, which are then stored on different machines/nodes
called shards. Each shard is a separate database instance that runs
on a separate machine. Each shard contains a subset of the data in
the overall dataset. Each shard is responsible for storing this subset
of the data and processing queries related to that subset.

MongoDB uses a sharded cluster architecture to manage sharding. A
sharded cluster consists of the following components:

1. Shard: A shard is a separate MongoDB instance on a separate
machine. Each shard is responsible for storing a subset of the data in
the dataset.

2. Router/Mongos: A router is a component that provides a single point of entry for client programs. Mongos acts as the interface between clients and the cluster. It receives queries from the client program and forwards them to the appropriate shards.

3. Config servers: Config servers store the metadata and configuration information for a sharded cluster.

MongoDB uses a technique called "Hashed Sharding" to distribute data equally among shards. It generates a hash value for every document and based on that hash value, it distributes the documents among shards. MongoDB can also use range-based sharding, where data is distributed based on a specific field's range, such as years, location, etc.

Sharding helps with scalability in MongoDB in the following ways:

1. Increased data distribution: Sharding allows MongoDB to distribute data across multiple machines, thus increasing data distribution and reducing data concentration, resulting in increased scalability.

2. Higher write throughput: Since the data is distributed over multiple shards, many writes can be executed in parallel, leading to a higher write throughput.

3. Improved query performance: Sharding the dataset allows the queries to be executed in parallel across multiple shards, which leads to improved query performance.

4. Better fault tolerance: By storing data across multiple machines, sharding provides fault tolerance. If one machine fails, the data is still available on other machines.

5. Reduced hardware costs: Sharding helps make better use of hardware resources by distributing the data across multiple commodity machines, which can reduce hardware costs.

Overall, sharding is a powerful technique that increases the scalability and performance of MongoDB. However, it comes with some complexity, such as managing multiple shards, configuring shards, and managing data distribution, which can create challenges in the initial setup and maintenance of the sharded cluster.

2.20   How do you perform a simple backup and restore operation in MongoDB?

Performing backups and restores in MongoDB is a crucial task when it comes to data management. MongoDB provides several tools to perform backups and restores that can be customized to suit specific needs. In this answer, I'll cover a simple backup and restore operation using the 'mongodump' and 'mongorestore' utilities.

Backup

The 'mongodump' utility is used to create backups of MongoDB databases. To create a backup of a database, execute the 'mongodump' command followed by the name of the database you want to backup:

```
mongodump --db <database_name>
```

For example, to create a backup of a database named 'mydatabase', the command would be:

```
mongodump --db mydatabase
```

This command creates a backup of the 'mydatabase' database in a directory named 'dump' in the current working directory.

You can also backup a single collection by specifying the '–collection' parameter:

```
mongodump --db <database_name> --collection <collection_name>
```

For example, to create a backup of a collection named 'mycollection' within the 'mydatabase' database, the command would be:

```
mongodump --db mydatabase --collection mycollection
```

This command creates a backup of the 'mycollection' collection in a directory named 'dump' in the current working directory.

You can also backup to a specific directory by specifying the '–out' parameter:

```
mongodump --db <database_name> --out <backup_directory>
```

For example, to create a backup of the 'mydatabase' database in a directory named 'mybackup', the command would be:

```
mongodump --db mydatabase --out mybackup
```

This command creates a backup of the 'mydatabase' database in a directory named 'mybackup' in the current working directory.

Restore

The 'mongorestore' utility is used to restore MongoDB database backups that were created using the 'mongodump' command. To restore a backup, execute the 'mongorestore' command followed by the path to the backup directory:

```
mongorestore <backup_directory>
```

For example, to restore a backup from a directory named 'mybackup', the command would be:

```
mongorestore mybackup
```

This command restores the 'mydatabase' database from the backup in the 'mybackup' directory.

You can also restore a single collection from a backup by specifying the '–collection' parameter:

```
mongorestore --db <database_name> --collection <collection_name> <
    backup_directory>/<collection_file>
```

For example, to restore a collection named 'mycollection' within the 'mydatabase' database from a backup in a directory named 'mybackup', the command would be:

```
mongorestore --db mydatabase --collection mycollection mybackup/mycollection.
    bson
```

This command restores the 'mycollection' collection from the 'mybackup/mycollection.bson' backup file.

Conclusion

In summary, performing backups and restores in MongoDB is essential for data management. The combination of 'mongodump' and 'mongorestore' is a straightforward way to create and restore back-ups. With this simple guide, one can execute a successful backup and restore operation.

Chapter 3

Intermediate

3.1 Explain the differences between embedded documents and references in MongoDB, and when to use each approach.

In MongoDB, embedding and referencing are two approaches to model relationships between collections.

Embedding is the practice of nesting one piece of data as a subdocument within another. For instance, consider a database containing collections of orders and products, where each order can contain multiple products. One way to model this would be to embed the product data directly within the order document, like this:

```
{
  "_id": ObjectId("5f7f6356fc19c6eca1d8c3c7"),
  "order_number": "ORD123",
  "customer_name": "John␣Doe",
  "products": [
    {
      "product_name": "Product␣A",
      "quantity": 2,
      "price": 25.99
    },
    {
      "product_name": "Product␣B",
      "quantity": 1,
```

```
    "price": 10.99
   }
 ]
}
```

Embedding can help with performance, as it eliminates the need for separate queries to retrieve related documents. It also simplifies the data model and can make it easier to work with the data. However, embedding can lead to data duplication and can make it more difficult to update related documents if they are embedded in multiple places.

Referencing, on the other hand, involves storing a reference to another document rather than embedding the entire document. For instance, in the example above, we could instead store the product data in a separate "products" collection and store references to those products in the order document:

```
{
  "_id": ObjectId("5f7f6356fc19c6eca1d8c3c7"),
  "order_number": "ORD123",
  "customer_name": "John Doe",
  "products": [
    ObjectId("5f7f63a0fc19c6eca1d8c3c8"),
    ObjectId("5f7f63a0fc19c6eca1d8c3c9")
  ]
}
```

With referencing, we avoid data duplication and can update related documents more easily. However, it requires additional queries to retrieve related data, which can impact performance.

When deciding whether to embed or reference related data in MongoDB, consider the following factors:

1. Data size: If the related data is small and straightforward, embedding may be a good option. However, if the related data is large or complex, referencing is likely a better choice.

2. Access patterns: If you frequently need to access related data along with the main document, embedding may be more efficient. However, if related data is only needed in certain cases, referencing may be more efficient overall.

3. Atomicity: If you need to update related data atomically (i.e. in a single database operation), referencing is the better choice, since updating an embedded document requires rewriting the entire main document.

In summary, embedding and referencing are both valid approaches to modeling relationships in MongoDB. The choice between the two depends on the specific requirements of your application.

3.2 What are the advantages of using the MongoDB ObjectId over a custom unique identifier for the _id field?

MongoDB uses an '_id' field to uniquely identify each document within a collection. By default, MongoDB generates and assigns a unique identifier of type 'ObjectId' to the '_id' field when a new document is inserted into a collection.

The advantages of using 'ObjectId' as opposed to a custom unique identifier for '_id' field in MongoDB are as follows:

1. **Uniqueness**: 'ObjectId' guarantees the uniqueness of the '_id' field. The probability of generating two 'ObjectId' values that are the same is practically zero, as they are generated using a combination of timestamp, machine identifier, and a unique sequence number. On the other hand, if a custom unique identifier is used, it is the application's responsibility to ensure its uniqueness.

2. **Efficiency**: MongoDB uses 'B-tree' indexes to store and retrieve data quickly. The tree structure of 'B-tree' indexes makes them efficient in querying and sorting data, especially when searching for ranges of values. Because 'ObjectId' values have a specific structure, the 'B-tree' index can efficiently store and search for documents based on their '_id' value.

3. **Easier to implement and maintain**: When using 'ObjectId' as the '_id' field, MongoDB automatically handles generating and assigning a unique identifier to each new document inserted into a collection. Moreover, 'ObjectId' is represented as a 12-byte hexadecimal string, which is easy to work with and maintain.

Example:

Consider a collection called 'users' which contains user data. Here is

an example of inserting a document into the 'users' collection with
an assigned 'ObjectId' value:

```
db.users.insertOne({
  _id: ObjectId("616ba1376c5d3bd3c49bda62"),
  name: "John␣Doe",
  age: 35,
  email: "johndoe@example.com"
});
```

In this example, we have assigned a custom 'ObjectId' value to the
'_id' field when inserting a new document into the 'users' collection.

Now, consider another scenario where we have used a custom unique
identifier instead of 'ObjectId'.

```
db.users.insertOne({
  _id: "JD-35-001",
  name: "John␣Doe",
  age: 35,
  email: "johndoe@example.com"
});
```

In this example, we have used a custom unique identifier of the format
'JD-35-001' as the '_id' field value. Although it ensures uniqueness
of the '_id' field, this approach has several disadvantages. Firstly,
we need to ensure that every identifier we create is unique and does
not already exist in the collection. Secondly, this approach is not
as computationally efficient as using 'ObjectId', as queries involving
sorting or searching for a specific range of '_id' values are less efficient.

Hence, in most cases, it is beneficial to use 'ObjectId' as opposed to
a custom unique identifier for the '_id' field in MongoDB.

3.3   How does MongoDB handle write and read concerns, and what are the different levels available?

MongoDB provides the flexibility to configure write and read operations according to the requirements of a specific application. MongoDB has four levels of write concern, and five levels of read concern,
which can be set on a per-operation basis, or can be set as the default
for the entire database or collection.

Write Concern

Write concerns determine the level of acknowledgment requested for write operations, which includes the number of replicas that need to acknowledge receipt of a write operation. In MongoDB, the available write concerns are:

- **w: 0**: This is the lowest level of acknowledgement, where a write operation does not wait for any acknowledgement from the replica set members. This write concern is useful for write operations that are not critical and where missing data is acceptable.

- **w: 1**: This is the default write concern, where a write operation waits for acknowledgement from the primary member of the replica set. This ensures that the data has been written to at least one member of the replica set.

- **w: majority**: A write operation waits for acknowledgement from the majority of the replica set members. This ensures that the data is written to a majority of the members, which makes it more durable and less prone to data loss in case of failures.

- **w: tag**: This write concern allows to specify an individual replica set tag or multiple tags with which to confirm that the write operation has propagated to the specific replica set members tagged with the corresponding values.

Example

Assuming we have a replica set comprising of three nodes 'NodeA, NodeB, and NodeC', we can set the write concern for a write operation as follows:

```
db.collection.insertOne(
  { name: "John", age: 35 },
  { writeConcern: { w: "majority" } }
);
```

This will wait for acknowledgment from the majority of replica set members before confirming that the operation is successful.

Read Concern

Read concerns determine the level of consistency required for read operations, which includes the number of replicas that should be read, and whether stale or unread data should be allowed. The available read concerns in MongoDB are:

- **local**: The read operation returns the most recent data available on the node handling the query, which may be stale data. This read concern is useful for read-intensive applications where data accuracy is not critical.

- **available**: The read operation returns the most recent data available from the replica set, and does not wait for any new data to be written. This read concern is useful for read-intensive applications where data accuracy is important but waiting for new data is not acceptable.

- **majority**: The read operation waits for data to be written to a majority of the replica set members and reads from the most up-to-date data available from the majority of the replica set members.

- **linearizable**: The read operation returns the most up-to-date data available from the replica set members, with a guarantee that any subsequent read operation will be guaranteed to see that data. This ensures that the data that is read is accurate and the latest version available.

- **snapshot**: The read operation returns data from a single point in time, preventing other write operations from interfering with the data read. The snapshot read concern is ideal for analytical queries.

Example

Assuming we have a replica set comprising of three nodes 'NodeA, NodeB, and NodeC', we can set the read concern for a read operation as follows:

```
db.collection.find(
    { name: "John" },
    { readConcern: { level: "majority" } }
);
```

This will wait for data to be written to a majority of the replica set members before returning the most up-to-date data available from the majority of the replica set members.

3.4   What is the role of MongoDB Compass, and how can it be used to interact with a MongoDB database?

MongoDB Compass is a graphical user interface (GUI) tool provided by the MongoDB for interacting with MongoDB databases. Its role is to provide an easy-to-use interface for developers, administrators, and other users to explore and manipulate MongoDB data with a wide variety of features and functionalities.

Here are some notable features of MongoDB Compass:

1. **Data exploration**: With MongoDB Compass, you can explore your data using GUI-based queries, which are very similar to the MongoDB query language. This feature allows developers to test out queries and see how they perform before running them in their code. Additionally, you can view documents and collections in a user-friendly way, which makes it easier to understand the structure of your data.

2. **Data manipulation**: MongoDB Compass allows you to add, edit, and delete documents, collections, and databases with just a few clicks. This feature is especially useful for those who are not comfortable with command-line interfaces.

3. **Schema visualization**: You can view your database schema and see how your data is structured without having to write any code. This is particularly helpful when you are working with large and complex datasets.

4. **Index management**: MongoDB Compass helps you create, modify, and delete indexes on your data. By optimizing indexes, you can increase the performance of your queries.

5. **Aggregation pipeline**: With MongoDB Compass, you can visualize and create aggregation pipelines, which allow you to perform complex data transformations and analysis on your data.

6. **Explain plan**: MongoDB Compass shows the query execution plan, which helps you understand how the MongoDB engine processes your queries.

To interact with a MongoDB database using MongoDB Compass, you need to follow these simple steps:

1. Install MongoDB Compass on your machine. You can download it from the MongoDB website.

2. Launch MongoDB Compass and connect to your database by providing the connection string or the necessary details such as hostname, port number, database name, and credentials.

3. Once you have connected to the database, you can view the documents and collections in the left pane of the interface. Selecting a collection opens the documents in the right pane.

4. You can perform different types of queries and manipulations by clicking on the corresponding button in the toolbar.

5. You can visualize the data using different types of charts and graphs available in MongoDB Compass.

6. You can use the aggregation pipeline editor to create and test complex aggregation queries.

7. Finally, you can export the data in different formats such as JSON, CSV, and BSON.

Here's an example of a relatively simple aggregation pipeline query that can be performed using MongoDB Compass:

```
db.customers.aggregate([
  { $match: { country: "USA" } },
  { $group: { _id: "$state", total_sales: { $sum: "$amount" } } },
  { $sort: { total_sales: -1 } }
])
```

This query retrieves all customers from the USA, groups them by state, calculates the total sales for each state, and finally, sorts them in descending order based on total sales.

In summary, MongoDB Compass is a powerful GUI tool that makes it easy to interact with MongoDB databases by providing a user-friendly interface for data exploration, manipulation, index management, schema visualization, aggregation pipeline, and explain plan.

3.5   Describe the process of creating and managing indexes in MongoDB.

Creating and managing indexes in MongoDB is an important aspect of performance tuning for the database. Indexes are used to speed up queries and make searches more efficient. MongoDB supports several types of indexes, including single-field, compound, geospatial, text, and hashed indexes.

To create an index in MongoDB, you can use the 'createIndex()'

method. This takes at least two arguments: the name of the collection to index and an object specifying the fields and options for the index. For example, to create a single-field index on the 'username' field of a collection named 'users', you would execute the following command:

```
db.users.createIndex({ username: 1 })
```

In this example, the '1' indicates that the index should be created in ascending order. To create a descending index, you would use '-1' instead.

You can also create compound indexes, which are indexes that span multiple fields. For example, to create a compound index on the 'city' and 'state' fields of a collection named 'locations', you would execute the following command:

```
db.locations.createIndex({ city: 1, state: 1 })
```

In addition to basic indexes, MongoDB also supports geospatial indexes for location-based searching and text indexes for full-text searching. To create a geospatial index on a field containing GeoJSON data, you would execute the following command:

```
db.places.createIndex({ location: "2dsphere" })
```

This creates a geospatial index called 'location' using the '2dsphere' option. Similarly, to create a text index on a collection's 'title' and 'description' fields, you would execute:

```
db.products.createIndex({ title: "text", description: "text" })
```

Once you've created an index, you can manage it using several methods. For example, you can view all of the indexes that exist on a collection using the 'getIndexes()' method, like so:

```
db.users.getIndexes()
```

This will return an array of index objects, including the name, keys, and options for each index.

You can also drop an index using the 'dropIndex()' method, like so:

```
db.users.dropIndex({ username: 1 })
```

This will remove the index on the 'username' field from the 'users'
collection.

In conclusion, creating and managing indexes in MongoDB is a straightforward process that involves using the 'createIndex()', 'getIndexes()',
and 'dropIndex()' methods to customize the indexing behavior of your
database. By creating optimal indexes and managing them effectively,
you can significantly improve the performance and efficiency of your
MongoDB queries.

3.6   How do you create and drop a unique index in MongoDB?

In MongoDB, an index is a data structure that improves the speed of
data retrieval operations. As its name implies, a unique index ensures
that the indexed field or fields contain unique values. This means that
no two documents in the collection can have the same value(s) for the
fields indexed with a unique index.

To create a unique index in MongoDB, you can use the 'createIndex()'
method on the collection object. The syntax of this method is as
follows:

```
db.collection.createIndex(keys, options)
```

The 'keys' parameter specifies the fields to include in the index and
their ordering. It should be an object that maps field names to their
sort order (1 for ascending, -1 for descending). For example:

```
db.myCollection.createIndex({ "name": 1 })
```

This creates a unique index on the 'name' field in the 'myCollection'
collection.

The 'options' parameter is an optional object that can be used to
specify additional options for the index. One of the options is 'unique',
which should be set to 'true' to create a unique index:

```
db.myCollection.createIndex({ "email": 1 }, { unique: true })
```

This creates a unique index on the 'email' field in the 'myCollection' collection.

To drop a unique index in MongoDB, you can use the 'dropIndex()' method on the collection object. The syntax of this method is as follows:

```
db.collection.dropIndex(index)
```

The 'index' parameter specifies the index to drop. It should be a string that identifies the index by name or an object that specifies the index keys. For example:

```
db.myCollection.dropIndex("name_1")
```

This drops the unique index on the 'name' field in the 'myCollection' collection.

Note that when you drop an index, you cannot undo the operation. The index and its metadata are permanently removed from the collection.

3.7   Explain the concept of index intersection in MongoDB.

Index intersection is a technique in MongoDB that allows to use more than one index to respond to a query, thus making the query more performant.

Normally, queries with multiple filter conditions may have to scan every document in a collection to find the appropriate results, which can be very slow for large collections. However, if we have multiple indexes that each cover parts of the query, we can perform an index intersection to achieve the same result.

For example, imagine we have a collection of books, and we want to find all the books that have been published after 2010 and that have a specific author. We could have separate indexes on the 'published_date' field and the 'author' field. MongoDB can then use both indexes to efficiently retrieve all documents that satisfy the query by using index intersection.

The following is an example of how index intersection works in a
MongoDB shell. Suppose we have a collection of cars that contains
the 'manufacturer', 'model', and 'year' fields.

```
> db.cars.createIndex({manufacturer: 1})
> db.cars.createIndex({model: 1})
> db.cars.createIndex({year: 1})
```

Now suppose we want to find all cars manufactured by Toyota, model
"Corolla", and produced after 2015. We can express this query as
follows:

```
> db.cars.find({
    manufacturer: "Toyota",
    model: "Corolla",
    year: {$gt: 2015}
  })
```

We can see that we could create a compound index on 'manufacturer: 1, model: 1, year: 1' that would cover this query. However,
suppose we only have the three individual indexes we created earlier. MongoDB can use index intersection to combine these indexes
to efficiently execute the query.

```
> db.cars.find({
    manufacturer: "Toyota",
    model: "Corolla",
    year: {$gt: 2015}
  })
  .hint("manufacturer_1_model_1_year_1")
```

In this example, we explicitly specify to the MongoDB query op-
timizer to use the compound index, even though we have separate
indexes. MongoDB then intersects the indexes to find the documents
that satisfy the query.

It is important to note that while index intersection can be useful, it
is not always the best option. Creating a compound index that covers
the query fields can often be more efficient, especially if the query is
very selective. Additionally, index intersection can add overhead to
the query if the indexes are not in memory. Therefore, as with any
performance optimization in MongoDB, it is important to test and
evaluate the most efficient approach for each use case.

3.8 What is the $lookup operator in the MongoDB aggregation framework, and how can it be used to perform a join-like operation?

The '$lookup' operator in the MongoDB aggregation framework is used to perform a left outer join between two collections in a MongoDB database. The operator retrieves matching documents from a "foreign" collection and adds them to the resulting documents from the primary collection.

The '$lookup' operator takes an object as its argument that specifies the foreign collection, specific local and foreign fields that need to match, the name of the array to which the result should be added, and any additional options.

Here's an example:

Suppose we have two collections in a database - orders and products. The orders collection contains an array of 'productIds' while the products collection has information about the products. We want to retrieve all the orders along with their corresponding products. We can achieve this using the '$lookup' operator as follows:

```
db.orders.aggregate([
    {
        $lookup: {
            from: "products",
            localField: "productIds",
            foreignField: "_id",
            as: "products"
        }
    }
])
```

In this example, the '$lookup' operation joins the orders collection with the products collection, matching the 'productIds' arrayin each document in the 'orders' collection with '_id' field in the 'products' collection.

The resulting output will contain the matched documents from products collection as an array field named 'products'.

```
{
```

```
"_id": ObjectId("6130c424a416f244e16a0dcb"),
"customer": "John␣Doe",
"productIds": [
    ObjectId("6130d67e7479190c69b9f9a7"),
    ObjectId("6130d6357479190c69b9f99c"),
    ObjectId("6130d6867479190c69b9f9a8")
],
"status": "delivered",
"products": [
    {
        "_id": ObjectId("6130d6357479190c69b9f99c"),
        "name": "Product␣A",
        "price": 10.5
    },
    {
        "_id": ObjectId("6130d67e7479190c69b9f9a7"),
        "name": "Product␣B",
        "price": 5.5
    },
    {
        "_id": ObjectId("6130d6867479190c69b9f9a8"),
        "name": "Product␣C",
        "price": 18.0
    }
]
}
```

In this result, we can see for every order document, the '$lookup'
operator searched for matching product documents and added them
to the 'products' field. If there was no match, the 'products' field
would simply be an empty array.

In summary, the '$lookup' operator is a powerful aggregation pipeline
tool that allows MongoDB to simulate a 'left outer join' operation
between two collections in the database. This operator can handle
complex queries with ease and is essential when working with related
documents in MongoDB databases.

3.9   How can you use the $unwind operator in the MongoDB aggregation framework?

The '$unwind' operator in MongoDB is used to deconstruct an array
field from the input documents to output a document for each element. This is particularly useful when we have documents with an
array field that we need to "flatten" for further processing.

The general syntax for the '$unwind' operator in MongoDB is as follows:

```
{
  $unwind: {
    path: "$<array_field>",
    includeArrayIndex: "<index_field>",
    preserveNullAndEmptyArrays: <boolean_value>
  }
}
```

where:

- '"array_field"' is the name of the array field that we want to deconstruct.

- '"index_field"' (optional) is the name of a new field to include the index of the array element. If not specified, the 'path' is a string, otherwise it is an object.

- '<boolean_value>' (optional) - when true, preserves the output array even when the input is null or empty, otherwise produces no output when the input is null or empty.

For example, consider the following MongoDB collection 'orders' where each document includes an array of 'items' ordered:

```
db.orders.insertMany([
{
  "_id": 1,
  "customer": "John",
  "items": [
    { "sku": "111", "qty": 2, "price": 10 },
    { "sku": "222", "qty": 1, "price": 20 }
  ]
},
{
  "_id": 2,
  "customer": "Jane",
  "items": [
    { "sku": "333", "qty": 5, "price": 5 },
    { "sku": "444", "qty": 10, "price": 1 }
  ]
}
])
```

If we want to calculate the total value of each order, we can use the '$unwind' operator to "flatten" the 'items' array and then perform a '$group' stage to calculate the total value for each order:

```
db.orders.aggregate([
  {
    $unwind: "$items"
  },
  {
    $group: {
      _id: "$_id",
      customer: { $first: "$customer" },
```

```
        total: { $sum: { $multiply: ["$items.qty", "$items.price"] } }
      }
   }
])
```

The output of this aggregation pipeline will be:

```
[
  { "_id": 1, "customer": "John", "total": 40 },
  { "_id": 2, "customer": "Jane", "total": 55 }
]
```

Note that we used the '$first' operator to keep the non-array fields ('_id' and 'customer') from the input documents in the output. We also used the '$multiply' operator to calculate the total value for each item by multiplying the quantity with the price.

Overall, the '$unwind' operator is a powerful and useful tool in the MongoDB aggregation framework when dealing with array fields.

3.10   What are some common aggregation pipeline stages in MongoDB, and what do they do?

MongoDB provides a powerful aggregation framework that enables users to process and analyze data using a set of pipeline stages. Here are some common aggregation pipeline stages in MongoDB:

1. **$match**: This stage filters documents based on specified conditions. It's similar to the 'find()' method where you can pass a query filter to retrieve documents from a collection.

Example: Suppose you have a collection of students and you want to retrieve all students who have a GPA greater than or equal to 3.5. This is how you would use the '$match' stage:

```
db.students.aggregate([
    { $match: { gpa: { $gte: 3.5 } } }
])
```

2. **$group**: This stage groups documents together based on a specified key and performs aggregate functions on each group.

Example: Let's say you want to calculate the average GPA for each major in your student collection. You can use the '$group' stage like this:

```
db.students.aggregate([
    { $group: { _id: "$major", avgGpa: { $avg: "$gpa" } } }
])
```

In this example, the '_$id' field specifies the key to group by, and '$avg' calculates the average GPA for each group.

3. **$project**: This stage reshapes documents by including, excluding, or transforming fields.

Example: Suppose you only want to retrieve the student name, major, and GPA from the previous example. You can use '$project' like this:

```
db.students.aggregate([
    { $group: { _id: "$major", avgGpa: { $avg: "$gpa" } } },
    { $project: { _id: 0, major: "$_id", avgGpa: 1 } }
])
```

In this example, '$project' excludes the '_id' field and renames the '_id' field to 'major'.

4. **$sort**: This stage sorts documents based on a specified field or fields.

Example: Suppose you want to sort the students in descending order of their GPA. You can use '$sort' like this:

```
db.students.aggregate([
    { $sort: { gpa: -1 } }
])
```

In this example, '-1' specifies descending order. If you want ascending order, you can use '1'.

5. **$limit**: This stage limits the number of documents in the pipeline.

Example: Suppose you only want to retrieve the top 10 students based on their GPA. You can use '$limit' like this:

```
db.students.aggregate([
    { $sort: { gpa: -1 } },
    { $limit: 10 }
])
```

In this example, '$sort' sorts students in descending order of their GPA and '$limit' restricts the pipeline to the top 10 students.

These are just a few common aggregation pipeline stages in MongoDB. There are many more stages available, such as '$unwind', '$lookup', '$addToSet', and more. The aggregation pipeline is a powerful and flexible tool for processing and analyzing data in MongoDB.

3.11 How can you create a capped collection in MongoDB, and what are its benefits and limitations?

A capped collection in MongoDB is a fixed-size collection that maintains insertion order. Once a capped collection reaches its maximum size, it overwrites the oldest documents with the newest ones. Creating a capped collection is fairly simple, just issue the 'createCollection()' command with the 'capped' option set to 'true', and specify the 'size' of the collection in bytes (or 'max' number of documents) as an optional parameter:

```
db.createCollection("my_capped_collection", { capped: true, size: 10000000 })
```

This creates a capped collection named 'my_capped_collection' that has a maximum size of 10 megabytes (in this case). The maximum number of documents is specified using the 'max' option.

The benefits of using a capped collection are:

- **Insertion order preservation**: Since documents are always written to the end of the collection and older documents are purged as new documents are added, a capped collection preserves the insertion order of its documents.

- **Automatic maintenance**: With the automatic purging of older documents, capped collections do not require any manual maintenance.

- **Fast writes**: Capped collections are designed to be highly efficient for write-heavy workloads. Inserting a new document is an O(1) operation, and updates to existing documents that do not increase the document size or require an index rebuild are similarly efficient.

The limitations of capped collections are:

- **Size limited**: The size of a capped collection is fixed and cannot be changed. When a capped collection reaches its maximum size, older documents are automatically purged to make room for new ones.

- **No updates to documents that would increase their size**: Once a document is inserted into a capped collection, you cannot update it in a way that would increase its size or require an index rebuild. If you try to do so, an error will be thrown.

- **No deletions or updates of individual documents by __id**: Because of the way capped collections are implemented, it is not possible to delete or update individual documents based solely on their '_id'. If you need to remove or modify a document, the only way to do so is to perform a query that returns it and then remove or update it as part of a bulk operation.

In general, capped collections are best used in situations where you need to store a fixed number of documents in a collection, and where you are primarily concerned with tracking the most recent documents that have been added. Some common use cases for capped collections include logging, real-time data processing, and message queues.

3.12 How do you perform pagination efficiently in MongoDB?

Pagination is a common operation in web applications that involve displaying a large set of data in smaller, more manageable pieces. When it comes to pagination in MongoDB, there are several methods to achieve efficient query performance depending on your data model and application requirements.

One of the most common strategies for pagination in MongoDB involves using the skip() and limit() methods. The skip() method lets you skip a specified number of documents, and the limit() method limits the number of results that are returned. Here is an example of using skip() and limit() for pagination:

```
db.collection.find().skip(pageNumber * pageSize).limit(pageSize)
```

In this example, we assume that pageNumber and pageSize are variables that represent the current page number and the number of documents to display per page, respectively. By multiplying the pageNumber by the pageSize, we can calculate the number of documents to skip before fetching the current page. Then, we limit the result set to pageSize documents.

While this strategy is straightforward, it can become inefficient as the number of pages grows large. Each skip() operation requires MongoDB to scan all the documents up to the specified skip value, which can lead to slower query performance. To avoid this limitation, you can make use of the cursor.skip() method instead of skip().

Here is an example of using cursor.skip() for pagination:

```
const cursor = db.collection.find();
cursor.skip(pageNumber * pageSize).limit(pageSize)
```

In this example, we retrieve a cursor from the collection, which allows us to process the results more efficiently. We then use cursor.skip() to skip the appropriate number of documents and cursor.limit() to limit the result set, just as we did with the previous example. The difference this time is that cursor.skip() can take advantage of index ordering to avoid scanning unnecessary documents, improving query performance.

Another strategy for pagination involves using the "range query" technique, where you specify a range of values for a query parameter (such as _id or timestamp) to retrieve a subset of documents. Here is an example of using the range query technique:

```
db.collection.find({_id: {$gt: lastId}}).limit(pageSize)
```

In this example, we assume that lastId is a variable that represents the last _id value from the previous page. By using the $gt operator, we can retrieve documents that have an _id greater than lastId, effectively "paginating" through the collection.

This technique works well when you have a well-defined and unique ordering criterion such as _id or timestamp. However, if you need to order by a custom field, you may need to create an index for that field to ensure efficient query performance.

In conclusion, there are several ways to perform efficient pagination in MongoDB. The most common strategies involve using skip() and limit() or cursor.skip() and cursor.limit() methods or range queries with a unique ordering criterion. By understanding the strengths and limitations of these techniques, you can choose the best approach for your application needs.

3.13 Explain the difference between the $push and $addToSet update operators.

Both $push and $addToSet are update operators in MongoDB which are used to add new elements to an array field. However, the key difference between these two update operators is how they handle inserting new elements into an array field.

The $push operator adds a specified value to an array field, even if it already exists in the array. If the specified value is an array itself, $push inserts the entire array as a single element of the main array. The syntax for using $push is as follows:

```
db.collection.update(
  <query>,
  { $push: { <field>: <value> } },
  { <options> }
)
```

Here, '<field>' is the array field to which the value is being pushed and '<value>' is the value being pushed. For example, consider the following query:

```
db.myCollection.update({"_id": ObjectId("5ea1ad2e284b54a77bcc97a4")}, {$push:
    {"scores": 80}})
```

This query finds a document with the specified '_id' and adds the value 80 to the 'scores' array, even if the array already contains the value 80.

On the other hand, the $addToSet operator adds a specified value to an array field only if it does not already exist in the array. If the specified value is an array itself, $addToSet checks if any element in the array already exists in the main array and only adds the entire array as a single element if none of its elements already exists. The syntax for using $addToSet is as follows:

```
db.collection.update(
  <query>,
  { $addToSet: { <field>: <value> } },
  { <options> }
)
```

Here, '<field>' is the array field to which the value is being added and '<value>' is the value being added. For example, consider the following query:

```
db.myCollection.update({"_id": ObjectId("5ea1ad2e284b54a77bcc97a4")}, {
    $addToSet: {"scores": 80}})
```

This query finds a document with the specified '_id' and adds the value 80 to the 'scores' array only if it does not already exist in the array.

To summarize, while both operators perform similar tasks of adding elements to an array field, the $push operator adds the element even if it already exists, while the $addToSet operator adds the element only if it does not already exist in the array.

3.14   What is a write concern "j:true" in MongoDB, and why is it important?

In MongoDB, write concern is the level of guarantee that a write operation was successfully committed to the database. A "j:true" write concern specifies that a write operation should only return when the data has been written to the journal.

MongoDB writes data to memory before persisting it to disk. In case of a catastrophic failure, such as power outage or system crash, any data written to memory but not yet persisted to disk can be lost. This is where the journal comes into play. The journal is a log that keeps track of any changes made to the database. Each write operation is recorded in the journal before being written to disk. In case of a catastrophic failure, MongoDB can use the journal to recover any data that was not yet persisted to disk.

With a write concern of "j:true", MongoDB ensures that the data is written to the database journal before returning success to the client. This provides an extra level of durability, as even in case of a catastrophic failure, the journal will be used to restore any lost data.

For example, consider the following code in Node.js that inserts a new document into a collection with write concern "j:true":

```
const MongoClient = require('mongodb').MongoClient;

const uri = "mongodb://localhost:27017/mydb";
const client = new MongoClient(uri);

client.connect(err => {
  const collection = client.db("mydb").collection("mycollection");
  const document = { name: "John", age: 30 };
  const options = { writeConcern: { j: true } };
  collection.insertOne(document, options, (err, res) => {
    console.log("Inserted document with _id:", res.insertedId);
    client.close();
  });
});
```

In this example, the insertOne() method is called with the options parameter specifying a write concern of "j:true". This ensures that the data is written to the journal before returning success to the client. The inserted document's _id value is then logged to the console.

In summary, a write concern of "j:true" is important in MongoDB to ensure that data is safely persisted to the journal, providing an extra layer of durability in case of a catastrophic failure.

3.15   Describe the process of horizontal scaling in MongoDB using sharding.

Horizontal scaling in MongoDB is achieved using sharding. Sharding is the process of distributing data across multiple servers, called shards, in order to improve performance and accommodate larger data sets. In this process, data is divided into small, manageable chunks and distributed across the shards.

To implement sharding in MongoDB, we need to follow the following steps:

1. Install and configure MongoDB: First, we need to install MongoDB

on each shard server and configure them to communicate with each other. We also need to enable sharding in the MongoDB configuration file.

2. Choose a sharding key: We need to choose a sharding key that represents the data that we want to distribute across the shards. The sharding key should be chosen based on the access patterns of the data and the size of the data set.

3. Enable sharding for the database: We need to enable sharding for the specific database that we want to shard. We can do this by connecting to the mongos instance and using the sh.enableSharding() command.

4. Create a sharded collection: Next, we need to create a sharded collection in the database. We can do this using the sh.shardCollection() command, which specifies the collection, sharding key and the number of shards to use.

5. Add shards: We need to add shards to the cluster using the sh.addShard() command, which specifies the hostname and port number of the shard server.

Once the above steps are completed, data will be automatically distributed across the shards based on the sharding key we have chosen. When a query is executed, the mongos instance will determine which shard contains the required data and route the query to that shard. The results are then aggregated and returned to the client.

For example, suppose we have a database of customer records with fields such as name, age, address and phone number. We can choose the age field as the sharding key since it is likely to be used in many queries and evenly distributed across the data set. We enable sharding for the database and create a sharded collection called customers using the age field as the sharding key. We add a few shards to the cluster and insert customer records into the customers collection. When a query is executed to find all customers with age greater than 30, the mongos instance routes the query to the shard containing the required data, aggregates the results and returns them to the client.

3.16   Explain the differences between hashed and ranged-based sharding in MongoDB.

Sharding is a process where data is distributed across multiple servers or nodes in a MongoDB cluster in order to improve performance and scalability. In MongoDB, there are two main types of sharding: hashed and ranged-based.

Hashed Sharding

In hashed sharding, a hash function is used to evenly distribute the data across the shards. The shard key value is input to the hash function, and the resulting hash value determines which shard the data should be stored on. This means that hashed sharding can help ensure even data distribution and prevent hotspots, as each shard gets an equal amount of data.

For example, let's say we have a database of customer information where the shard key is the customer's last name. With hashed sharding, the last name would be input to a hash function, which would generate a hash value that determines which shard the data should be stored on. This means that all customer data would be evenly distributed across the shards.

While hashed sharding can help ensure even data distribution and prevent hotspots, it can make querying a bit more difficult, as queries that rely on the shard key can be slower due to the data being spread out across multiple shards.

Range-based Sharding

In ranged-based sharding, data is divided into ranges based on the shard key. Each shard is responsible for a specific range of values based on the shard key. This means that data that falls within a certain range will always be stored on the same shard.

For example, let's say we have a database of hotel reservations where the shard key is the reservation date. With range-based sharding, we could divide the reservations into monthly ranges and assign each range to a specific shard. This means that all reservations for a specific month would always be stored on the same shard.

Range-based sharding can make querying faster, as queries that rely on the shard key can be executed on a single shard. However, it can lead to hotspots if data is not evenly distributed across the ranges or if new data is added to an already full range.

In summary, hashed sharding can help ensure even data distribution and prevent hotspots but can make querying a bit more difficult, while range-based sharding can make querying faster but can lead to hotspots if data is not evenly distributed. The choice between the two types of sharding largely depends on the specific use case and the characteristics of the data being stored.

3.17   What is the role of a MongoDB config server in a sharded cluster?

In MongoDB, a sharded cluster is a set of MongoDB instances, called shards, that work together to hold a large data set. The data in a sharded cluster is partitioned into smaller, manageable parts called chunks that are distributed across the shards. The shards are responsible for storing and retrieving chunks of data from the data set.

To support sharding, MongoDB uses a configuration server that stores metadata about the sharded cluster, such as information about the shards, chunks, and mappings between chunk ranges and shards. The configuration server acts as a central repository for cluster-wide metadata and is responsible for coordinating the activities of the shards.

In a sharded cluster, each MongoDB instance operates in one of three roles: a shard, a config server, or a mongos server.

The role of a config server in a sharded cluster is to manage and distribute cluster metadata. More specifically, the config server stores metadata about the mapping of chunks to shards, as well as configuration data for the cluster, such as the location of the shards, the collections that are sharded, and the routing rules for queries.

When a client submits a query to a mongos server, the mongos server uses the metadata from the config server to determine the appropriate shard(s) to send the query to. The config server also receives and serves requests from the shards for information about the cluster configuration, such as information about ranges of chunks or the location of specific data records.

In summary, the role of a MongoDB config server in a sharded cluster is to store and manage metadata about the sharded data, providing the necessary information to the mongos server to route data to the correct shards.

3.18 How do you monitor and optimize MongoDB performance?

MongoDB is a NoSQL document-oriented database that stores data in the form of documents in BSON format (Binary JSON). It is a high-performance database that provides scalability and flexibility, but to achieve maximum performance, it is essential to monitor and optimize its performance regularly. In this answer, we will discuss various tools and techniques that can be used to monitor and optimize MongoDB performance.

Monitoring MongoDB Performance To monitor MongoDB performance, we can use various tools and techniques such as:

1. MongoDB Profiler The MongoDB Profiler is an excellent tool to monitor and analyze the performance of a MongoDB database. It tracks the queries that MongoDB executes and provides useful information such as the execution time, the number of examined documents, and the indexes used in the query.

To enable the profiler, we can use the 'db.setProfilingLevel()' method, which takes a numeric argument that indicates the level of profiling. There are three levels of profiling:

'0': Profiling is off.

'1': Profiling is on for slow operations only. It records operations that take more than a specified time to execute.

'2': Profiling is on for all operations.

Once the profiler is enabled, we can use the 'db.system.profile' collection to access the profiling data. We can query this collection and get insights into the queries that are taking longer to execute.

2. MongoDB Monitoring Service (MMS) MongoDB Monitoring Service (MMS) is a free monitoring tool for MongoDB that helps us visualize and analyze the performance of our MongoDB clusters. This tool provides a graphical representation of the health and performance of the clusters, including CPU usage, memory usage, disk usage, and network activity.

MMS also provides alerts for critical events and performance metrics that exceed predefined thresholds. It integrates well with other monitoring and alerting tools, making it an excellent tool for monitoring large and complex MongoDB environments.

3. Operating System Tools Monitoring the operating system is equally essential to monitor MongoDB performance. Techniques such as monitoring system metrics like CPU usage, disk usage, and memory usage can help us understand and analyze the impact of MongoDB on the system resources.

We can use various system-level tools such as 'top', 'htop', 'vmstat', and 'iostat' to monitor system metrics. These tools can help us identify high CPU utilization, memory usage, and disk I/O latency issues related to MongoDB.

Optimizing MongoDB Performance

To optimize MongoDB performance, we can use various techniques such as:

1. Indexing Indexing plays a crucial role in optimizing MongoDB performance. Creating appropriate indexes can significantly improve the efficiency of queries and reduce query latency. When dealing with large datasets, creating indexes on fields that are frequently used in queries can be a game-changer.

There are different types of indexes in MongoDB, such as Single Field Indexes, Compound Indexes, Text Indexes, Geospatial Indexes, and Hashed Indexes. We should choose the appropriate index type based on the nature of the data and the queries we are executing.

2. Sharding Sharding is a technique used to horizontally scale MongoDB by distributing data across multiple servers. This technique helps in increasing the throughput of reads and writes, decreasing query latency, and handling large datasets.

To implement sharding, we need to have a sharded cluster with at least two pieces of a replica set. We then choose a sharding key and enable sharding on the database/collection that we want to shard. MongoDB automatically distributes the data across the shards based on the chosen sharding key.

3. Aggregation Framework The Aggregation Framework is an excellent tool to optimize MongoDB performance when dealing with complex queries. This framework allows us to perform complex data transformations, data filtering, and data analysis in a single query.

The Aggregation Framework processes the data in-memory, making it faster while reducing I/O operations. It provides a set of pipeline stages such as '$match', '$group', '$project', '$sort', and many others, that we can use to optimize the query performance.

4. Capped Collections Capped Collections are collections with a fixed size that automatically overwrites the oldest entries with new ones when the collections reach their maximum size. These collections are perfect for scenarios where real-time data is being ingested and queried frequently.

Since Capped Collections are limited in size, they are faster than regular collections. They also ensure that the database size does not grow indefinitely, reducing the chance of disk space-related issues.

5. Write Concern and Write Acknowledgment When inserting data into a MongoDB database, we can set the write concern and write acknowledgment levels to optimize MongoDB's write performance. Write acknowledgment determines whether MongoDB should wait for a confirmation of a write from the primary or secondary node before reporting a write operation as successful to the application.

Higher the level of write acknowledgment, the slower the write operations. By setting 'w' to 0 and 'j' to false, we can speed up the write operations at a cost of durability.

To summarize, monitoring and optimizing MongoDB performance is crucial for large, complex databases that must perform consistently and efficiently. By using tools like MongoDB profiler, MMS, and operating system tools and techniques like indexing, sharding, aggregation frameworks, capped collections, write concern and write acknowledgment, we can significantly improve MongoDB's performance.

3.19   What are some MongoDB security best practices?

MongoDB is one of the most popular NoSQL databases out there, used by a large number of organizations all around the world. Since these databases often contain sensitive data, it's important to ensure that they're kept secure from any malicious activity, unauthorized access, or data breaches. In this regard, let's discuss some of the best security practices for MongoDB.

1. Use Authentication: MongoDB should always be configured to require authentication. This can be done easily by setting up authentication in MongoDB configuration files. Authentication will ensure that only authorized users can access the database.

2. Apply Encryption: Encryption is another important security best practice that can secure your MongoDB database. SSL/TLS encryption should be used to protect network traffic between client applications and MongoDB clusters. Transparent Data Encryption (TDE) can also be used to protect data at rest.

3. Limit Network Exposure: Limiting network exposure is essential to prevent malicious actors from exploiting vulnerabilities in open network ports. It is best to configure MongoDB to listen only on local network interfaces. Use appropriate firewalls to restrict incoming and outgoing network traffic.

4. Keep MongoDB Updated: New versions of MongoDB are released frequently, and it's important to keep your MongoDB installation up-to-date to ensure that known security issues are patched promptly.

5. Restrict MongoDB Operations: Expose only necessary operations that client applications require. MongoDB has a rich set of tools and

commands that can be used to restrict specific database operations by creating custom roles and setting up authorization with custom permissions.

6. Avoid Default Settings: MongoDB has default settings that may not meet your security needs. You should always carefully evaluate them and adjust them to fit your particular security requirements.

7. Regularly Back up Your Data: Regular data backups should be a part of any database security plan. In case of a data breach or failure, you will have a recent backup of your data.

8. Assign Proper User Roles: Assign roles to users with the least privileges required for their specific tasks.

Applying above security best practices won't guarantee that your MongoDB database is invulnerable to attacks or accidental data loss, but it would minimize the risks associated with it. Security should always be a top priority for MongoDB administrators.

3.20   Explain the differences between MongoDB Community Edition and MongoDB Enterprise Edition.

MongoDB is an open source NoSQL document-oriented database system that is designed to store, query and access data in a highly scalable and flexible way. MongoDB offers two main editions which include the Community Edition and the Enterprise Edition. In this response, we will discuss the differences between these two editions.

MongoDB Community Edition

MongoDB Community Edition is the free and open source version of MongoDB which is available to be used by anyone. It provides all the main features of MongoDB such as document storage, indexing and querying, aggregation, replication, and sharding. It is widely used by developers, startups and small businesses because it is free and provides a great way to get started with MongoDB.

Features of MongoDB Community Edition include:

1. Free to use: MongoDB Community Edition is free to download and use.

2. Open Source: The source code for MongoDB Community Edition is available to anyone and can be modified and distributed under the AGPL license.

3. Document-oriented: MongoDB is a document-oriented database system which is designed to work well with JSON-style document data.

4. Scalability: MongoDB Community Edition provides a highly scalable architecture that allows you to scale horizontally by adding more nodes to your cluster.

5. High Availability: MongoDB Community Edition provides automatic replication and failover to ensure high availability and data durability.

6. Security: MongoDB Community Edition provides security features such as access controls, authentication, and encryption.

MongoDB Enterprise Edition

MongoDB Enterprise Edition is the commercial version of MongoDB which offers additional features that are not available in the Community Edition. It is designed for larger organizations that require additional capabilities such as advanced security features, support for compliance standards, and additional tools for management and monitoring. The Enterprise Edition is available in three different tiers which include Standard, Advanced, and Premium.

Features of MongoDB Enterprise Edition include:

1. Advanced Security Features: MongoDB Enterprise Edition provides advanced security features such as LDAP and Kerberos Authentication, Encrypted Storage Engine, and auditing to comply with regulatory requirements.

2. Support for Compliance Standards: MongoDB Enterprise Edition supports various compliance standards such as HIPAA, PCI DSS, and

SOC 2.

3. Management and Monitoring: MongoDB Enterprise Edition provides a set of enterprise-level features for management and monitoring such as MongoDB Management Service, MongoDB Ops Manager and Cloud Manager.

4. Integrations with Other Tools: MongoDB Enterprise Edition provides integrations with various other tools such as Hadoop, Spark, and Tableau.

5. Support: MongoDB Enterprise Edition provides support from MongoDB experts and engineers to help users with any problems they may face.

In summary, MongoDB Community Edition is great for startups, small businesses, and developers who want to use the database platform for free. However, if you are part of a larger organization or require additional features such as compliance certifications, advanced security features, or more advanced management and monitoring options, then the MongoDB Enterprise Edition may be the better choice.

Chapter 4

Advanced

4.1 How does the MongoDB storage engine WiredTiger differ from the older MMAPv1, and what are the advantages of using WiredTiger?

WiredTiger and MMAPv1 are both storage engines supported by MongoDB. However, they differ in terms of their architecture, data compression, concurrency control, and journaling approach.

MMAPv1 stores data on disk as memory-mapped files, which means that the data is mapped into virtual memory and accessed directly from disk by the process. This approach provides high performance but can be limited in terms of scalability and concurrency. On the other hand, WiredTiger uses a document-level locking approach that allows for more fine-grained concurrency control, making it more scalable in multi-threaded environments.

One of the main advantages of WiredTiger is its support for compression. WiredTiger allows for data to be compressed when written to disk, which reduces the amount of disk space needed for storing data. WiredTiger uses compression algorithms such as Snappy, zlib, and bzip2, and can compress data up to 80

Another advantage of WiredTiger is its support for multi-document transactions. WiredTiger allows multiple operations to be grouped into transactions, making it easier to ensure data consistency across a distributed system. This feature can be helpful when implementing complex business logic that spans multiple documents.

WiredTiger also provides a more efficient journaling approach than MMAPv1. In MMAPv1, the journal simply logs changes to the database, while WiredTiger maintains a separate file for its journal that is compressed and rotated periodically. This approach provides better durability and reduces I/O latency for write operations.

Finally, WiredTiger provides better compression and encryption capabilities than MMAPv1. WiredTiger's encryption approach is pluggable, meaning that users can choose their own encryption algorithm and key management system.

In summary, WiredTiger provides a more scalable, efficient, and secure approach to data storage than MMAPv1, with support for compression, multi-document transactions, and pluggable encryption.

4.2 Explain the concept of Journaling in MongoDB and its importance in ensuring data durability.

Journaling in MongoDB is a process of recording write operations that occur on a database to a separate, persistent file called a journal before they are written to the actual data files. This is an important feature of MongoDB that helps ensure data durability, which is the ability of a system to recover data after a failure, such as a power outage or other unexpected events.

MongoDB uses a write-ahead log (WAL) to capture all write operations made against the database. Every time a write operation is performed, it is recorded in an in-memory data structure called the oplog. The oplog consists of a series of instructions that MongoDB uses to restore the state of a database to a consistent state in the event of a failure. These instructions are called "oplog entries".

The oplog entries are then written to the journal file, which is a binary file on disk. The Journal file is a sequential, circular buffer that conserves the most recent changes made to MongoDB's data files. The journal file is small in comparison to the data files and it writes quickly due to this sequential approach. Once the data is written to the journal file, it can be written lazily to disk at a later point in time when the system has enough resources to commit data to disk safely.

The importance of journaling in MongoDB is that it provides an additional level of data protection. By capturing operations in the journal before writing them to the data files, MongoDB ensures that if a failure occurs, any uncommitted write operations are not lost. When MongoDB restarts, it can use the oplog entries stored in the journal file to recover any uncommitted writes and restore the database to its previous state.

In addition, journaling helps to improve write performance by allowing MongoDB to perform writes asynchronously, since MongoDB can write operations to the in-memory oplog immediately, without waiting for them to be written to disk. This improves the overall performance of MongoDB, especially in high-write workloads.

In conclusion, journaling is an important feature of MongoDB that provides data durability by capturing all write operations in a separate persistent file before writing them to the data files. This ensures that any uncommitted writes are not lost in the event of a failure and allows MongoDB to recover data quickly and efficiently.

4.3 How do you manage large files in MongoDB using GridFS, and what are its benefits?

MongoDB provides a feature called GridFS to store and manage large files efficiently. Instead of storing large files in a single document, GridFS divides the file into multiple parts, called chunks, and stores each chunk as a separate document. It also stores metadata about the file, such as the filename, content type, and file size, in a separate document called the files collection.

To use GridFS, you first need to create a connection to your MongoDB database and initialize a GridFS bucket. In Python, you can do this using the following code:

```
from pymongo import MongoClient
from gridfs import GridFS

client = MongoClient('localhost', 27017)
db = client['my_database']
fs = GridFS(db, collection='my_files')
```

Once you have initialized the GridFS bucket, you can use its methods to store and retrieve files. To store a file in GridFS, you can use the 'put()' method, as shown below:

```
with open('large_file.pdf', 'rb') as f:
    file_id = fs.put(f, filename='large_file.pdf', content_type='application/
        pdf')
    print(file_id)
```

This will upload the file 'large_file.pdf' to GridFS and return the unique identifier assigned to the file. The metadata about the file, including the filename and content type, is also stored in the files collection.

To retrieve a file from GridFS, you can use the 'get()' method, as shown below:

```
import io

file_id = ObjectId('60cde9c450ef306f1bacb99a')
f = fs.get(file_id)
content = f.read()
```

This will retrieve the file with the specified ID from GridFS and return it as a file object, which can be read using Python's standard I/O functions. Note that the file is retrieved in chunks, and the 'read()' method returns the concatenated contents of all the chunks.

One of the major benefits of using GridFS to manage large files in MongoDB is that it allows you to store files larger than the 16 MB size limit for BSON documents. GridFS automatically divides the file into chunks and stores each chunk as a separate document, allowing you to store files of virtually any size. Additionally, because GridFS stores metadata about the file separately from the chunks themselves, it enables you to efficiently query and retrieve files based on their attributes, such as filename or content type.

Another benefit of GridFS is that it provides a standardized way to store and retrieve large files in MongoDB, making it easy to integrate with other tools and applications that rely on MongoDB for data storage. For example, you could use GridFS to store video files for a web application, and then use MongoDB's aggregation and indexing capabilities to search and filter the files based on their metadata.

In summary, GridFS provides a powerful and flexible mechanism for managing large files in MongoDB, allowing you to store files of virtually any size and leverage MongoDB's rich querying and indexing capabilities to efficiently search and retrieve them.

4.4   What are the various strategies to model tree structures in MongoDB, and when should you use each approach?

Tree structures can be modeled in MongoDB using various approaches. The choice of approach depends on the requirements of the application and the queries that need to be performed on the tree data.

1. Parent References:
One common approach is to use the parent-reference model, where each document represents a node in the tree and contains a reference to its parent node. This approach is similar to the way trees are represented in file systems. The parent-reference model makes it easy to traverse the tree upwards, but querying children or descendants requires multiple queries or recursive functions.

Example: Consider a simple folder structure, where each folder contains a list of subfolders:

```
{
  "_id": ObjectId("61528a2850d93b46505a76e5"),
  "name": "Folder␣A",
  "parent": null,
  "children": [
    ObjectId("61528a2850d93b46505a76e7"),
    ObjectId("61528a2850d93b46505a76e8")
  ]
}
{
  "_id": ObjectId("61528a2850d93b46505a76e7"),
  "name": "Folder␣A1",
```

```
  "parent": ObjectId("61528a2850d93b46505a76e5"),
  "children": []
}

{
  "_id": ObjectId("61528a2850d93b46505a76e8"),
  "name": "Folder␣A2",
  "parent": ObjectId("61528a2850d93b46505a76e5"),
  "children": [
    ObjectId("61528a2850d93b46505a76e9")
  ]
}

{
  "_id": ObjectId("61528a2850d93b46505a76e9"),
  "name": "Folder␣A21",
  "parent": ObjectId("61528a2850d93b46505a76e8"),
  "children": []
}
```

2. Child References:

Another approach is to use the child-reference model, where each document contains a reference to its immediate child or children. This makes traversing down the tree easy, but querying upstream nodes requires multiple queries or recursive functions.

Example: Consider a simple folder structure, where each folder contains a reference to its immediate child folder:

```
{
  "_id": ObjectId("61528d9250d93b46505a76ea"),
  "name": "Folder␣A",
  "child": ObjectId("61528d9250d93b46505a76ec")
}

{
  "_id": ObjectId("61528d9250d93b46505a76ec"),
  "name": "Folder␣A1",
  "child": null
}

{
  "_id": ObjectId("61528d9250d93b46505a76ed"),
  "name": "Folder␣A2",
  "child": ObjectId("61528d9250d93b46505a76ef")
}

{
  "_id": ObjectId("61528d9250d93b46505a76ef"),
  "name": "Folder␣A21",
  "child": null
}
```

3. Materialized Paths:

The materialized path approach uses a text field in each document to store the full path to the document. This path includes the IDs of all ancestors, separated by a delimiter. This makes it easy to query all descendants or ancestors of a node using indexed regular expression patterns. However, updating the path of all descendants when a node is moved in the tree can be expensive.

Example: Consider a simple folder structure, where each folder contains a string 'path' field:

```
{
  "_id": ObjectId("61528f4450d93b46505a76f0"),
  "name": "Folder␣A",
  "path": "/",
}

{
  "_id": ObjectId("61528f4450d93b46505a76f1"),
  "name": "Folder␣A1",
  "path": "/61528f4450d93b46505a76f0/",
}

{
  "_id": ObjectId("61528f4450d93b46505a76f2"),
  "name": "Folder␣A2",
  "path": "/61528f4450d93b46505a76f0/",
}

{
  "_id": ObjectId("61528f4450d93b46505a76f3"),
  "name": "Folder␣A21",
  "path": "/61528f4450d93b46505a76f0/61528f4450d93b46505a76f2/",
}
```

4. Nested Sets:
The nested set approach uses two numeric fields in each document to store the range of descendent nodes in the tree. This makes it easy to query all descendants or ancestors of a node, but updating the range of all descendant nodes when a node is moved in the tree can be expensive.

Example: Consider a simple folder structure, where each folder contains 'lft' (left) and 'rgt' (right) fields:

```
{
  "_id": ObjectId("615292d750d93b46505a76f4"),
  "name": "Folder␣A",
  "lft": 1,
  "rgt": 6
}

{
  "_id": ObjectId("615292d750d93b46505a76f5"),
  "name": "Folder␣A1",
  "lft": 2,
  "rgt": 3
}

{
  "_id": ObjectId("615292d750d93b46505a76f6"),
```

```
  "name": "Folder␣A2",
  "lft": 4,
  "rgt": 5
}

{
  "_id": ObjectId("615292d750d93b46505a76f7"),
  "name": "Folder␣A21",
  "lft": 5,
  "rgt": 6
}
```

In summary, different approaches to model tree structures in MongoDB have different strengths and weaknesses. Applications should consider the requirements for querying the tree data in order to choose the appropriate approach.

4.5 How do you handle transactions in MongoDB, and what are the limitations?

MongoDB supports multi-document transactions starting from version 4.0. With transactions, users can perform multiple insert, update, or delete operations on multiple collections and have them either all succeed or all fail, preserving the integrity of the data. Transactions are commonly used in scenarios that involve multiple databases or multiple collections within a database. Transactions can be managed using the following objects in MongoDB:

1. 'ClientSession': A session object that MongoDB uses to store transaction-specific data, such as transaction ID.

2. 'TransactionOptions': An object that sets transaction options, such as read concern and write concern.

3. 'Transaction': An object that specifies the sequence of database operations to be performed within a transaction.

To execute a transaction in MongoDB, you need to follow these steps:

1. Begin a session.

2. Start a transaction using the session.

3. Perform multiple read and write operations within the transaction using the session.

4. Commit or abort the transaction.

Here is an example code snippet that demonstrates how to use transactions in MongoDB:

```
// Begin a session
session = client.startSession();
session.startTransaction();

try {
  // Read and write operations within the transaction
  session.getDatabase("db1").getCollection("coll1").insertOne(new Document("
      _id", "doc1"));
  session.getDatabase("db2").getCollection("coll2").updateOne(new Document("
      _id", "doc2"),
  new Document("$set", new Document("field1", "value1")));

  // Commit the transaction
  session.commitTransaction();
} catch (RuntimeException e) {
  // Abort the transaction if there is an error
  session.abortTransaction();
} finally {
  // End the session
  session.close();
}
```

However, there are some limitations that come with using Mongo transactions. These limitations are:

1. Distributed transactions cannot be performed across shards in a MongoDB cluster.

2. The transaction cannot operate on more than 1000 documents.

3. MongoDB does not support nested transactions.

4. Transactions increase the load on the server and may affect performance when they are used excessively.

5. Transactions cannot be used with certain write operations such as 'geoNear'.

In conclusion, MongoDB supports transactions to ensure data integrity when performing multiple read and write operations. However, there are certain limitations that come with using transactions, such as performance, scalability, and the inability to perform distributed transactions across shards.

4.6   Explain the process of creating and managing compound indexes in MongoDB.

Compound indexes in MongoDB allow users to create indexes on multiple fields within a single collection. This can greatly improve query performance for operations that involve multiple fields in a query or sort. In this answer, we will go through the process of creating and managing compound indexes in MongoDB.

Creating a Compound Index To create a compound index, we can call the createIndex() method on the collection and pass in an object that specifies the fields to be indexed and the order of their precedence. Here's an example:

```
db.collection.createIndex({ field1: 1, field2: -1 })
```

In this example, we are creating a compound index on field1 and field2, with field1 having ascending order (-1 means descending order).

Managing a Compound Index We can check if an index exists on a collection by calling getIndexes() method on the collection. Here's the command to do that:

```
db.collection.getIndexes()
```

This will return an array of objects, each representing an index on the collection. We can also drop an index using the dropIndex() method. Here's an example:

```
db.collection.dropIndex("field1_1_field2_-1")
```

Here, we are dropping the index on field1 and field2 we created earlier, which has an index name of "field1_1_field2_-1". We can also drop all indexes on a collection using the dropIndexes() method. This will remove all indexes and build a new, default index on the _id field. Here's an example:

```
db.collection.dropIndexes()
```

This will drop all indexes on the collection.

Conclusion

In conclusion, compound indexes in MongoDB allow for improved query performance by allowing indexing on multiple fields. This increases read performance by returning results faster. Creating and managing these indexes are simple and can significantly improve query performance for large collections. Proper use of indexes in MongoDB is a key step in optimizing database performance.

4.7 What is a covered query in MongoDB, and how does it improve performance?

In MongoDB, a covered query is a query that is able to fully utilize an index to retrieve all necessary data without having to evaluate documents. Specifically, a covered query means that all the fields required for projection or sorting are contained within the index keys, and there is no need to fetch additional documents from disk to satisfy these operations.

When a covered query is executed, MongoDB can utilize the index's compact structure to retrieve only the data needed for the query without requiring additional scanning of the entire collection. This has a significant impact on the performance of the query.

For example, let's consider the following query:

```
db.users.find({age: {$gt: 18}}, {_id: 0, name: 1, age: 1}).sort({age: 1})
```

If there is a compound index on 'age' and 'name', that includes all the fields in the query, then this query can be fully satisfied by the index, and there's no need for MongoDB to evaluate any documents.

In contrast, if there is no appropriate index, MongoDB would have to scan the entire collection to evaluate each document, and then sort and project as needed. This can be very slow, especially if the collection is large.

Thus, covering queries can improve the performance of MongoDB queries by minimizing the amount of data that needs to be pulled from the disk and boosting query speeds when used appropriately.

4.8   How do you use the $facet operator in the MongoDB aggregation framework to process multiple pipelines?

The $facet operator in the MongoDB aggregation framework is used to process multiple pipelines within a single stage. The $facet operator facilitates the execution of multiple aggregation pipelines within a single stage in the aggregation pipeline. The output from each sub-pipeline is returned as a named field in the output document.

Here is the basic syntax of the $facet operator:

```
{
  $facet: {
    <outputField1>: [ <aggregationPipeline1> ],
    <outputField2>: [ <aggregationPipeline2> ],
    ...
  }
}
```

In this syntax, the $facet operator takes an object that has multiple keys, with each key representing the name of the sub-pipeline that we want to execute. The value of each key is an array, and each element of the array represents one stage of the pipeline for the sub-pipeline.

Here's an example that demonstrates the usage of the $facet operator. Let's say we have a collection named "orders" that contains documents representing orders from an online retailer. Each order document contains fields such as the customer ID, order date, and order total.

Suppose we want to get the total revenue generated by the retailer in a given month, broken down by customer. We can use the $facet operator to execute two pipelines in parallel: one that groups the orders by customer ID and calculates the total revenue generated by each customer, and another that groups the orders by month and calculates the total revenue for each month. Here is how we can do this:

```
db.orders.aggregate([
  {
    $match: {
      orderDate: {
        $gte: ISODate('2021-01-01'),
        $lte: ISODate('2021-01-31')
      }
    }
  },
  {
    $facet: {
      "byCustomer": [
        {
          $group: {
            _id: "$customerId",
            revenue: { $sum: "$orderTotal" }
          }
        }
      ],
      "byMonth": [
        {
          $group: {
            _id: { $month: "$orderDate" },
            revenue: { $sum: "$orderTotal" }
          }
        }
      ]
    }
  }
])
```

In this example, we start by using a $match stage to filter the orders that were placed in the month of January 2021. Then, we use the $facet operator to execute two sub-pipelines in parallel. The "by-Customer" sub-pipeline uses the $group stage to group the orders by customer ID and calculate the total revenue generated by each customer. The "byMonth" sub-pipeline uses the $group stage to group the orders by month and calculate the total revenue generated in each month.

The output of the aggregation pipeline will be an array with one document, containing two fields - "byCustomer" and "byMonth". The value of each field will be an array with one document for each customer and each month, respectively, with the "_id" field containing the customer ID or the month number, and the "revenue" field containing the corresponding revenue. For example:

```
[
  {
    "byCustomer": [
      { "_id": "customer123", "revenue": 550 },
      { "_id": "customer456", "revenue": 250 },
      ...
    ],
    "byMonth": [
```

```
    { "_id": 1, "revenue": 1800 }
   ]
  }
 ]
```

In this output, we can see that customer123 generated $550 in revenue
in January 2021, customer456 generated $250 in revenue in January
2021, and the retailer generated a total of $1800 in revenue in January
2021.

4.9   Explain the concept of data consistency in MongoDB, and how it's affected by the write concern and read preference settings.

Data consistency refers to the accuracy and reliability of the data
stored in a MongoDB database. In other words, it ensures that all
replicas of the data are in synchronization and any changes made
to the data are reflected consistently across all replicas. MongoDB
provides several options to control data consistency, including write
concern and read preference settings.

Write concern is a mechanism that determines the level of acknowledgement required from MongoDB after a write operation is performed. It specifies the number of replicas that must acknowledge
the write operation before it is considered successful. The different
write concern levels that can be set are:

- `w: 0`: No acknowledgement is required. The write operation is considered
  successful even if it fails on the server.
- `w: 1`: Acknowledgement is required from the primary replica. The write
  operation is considered successful if it is successful on the primary
  replica.
- `w: majority`: Acknowledgement is required from the majority of the
  replicas. The write operation is considered successful only if it is
  successful on the majority of the replicas.

The write concern level affects data consistency because it determines
how many replicas need to acknowledge a write operation before it
is considered successful. A higher write concern level ensures higher
consistency because it requires more replicas to acknowledge the write
operation before it is considered successful.

Read preference is a mechanism that determines from which replicas
clients read data. It specifies the preferred replicas to read data from
based on the availability and consistency of the data. The different
read preference modes that can be set are:

```
- `primary`: Clients read data only from the primary replica.
- `primaryPreferred`: Clients prefer to read data from the primary replica,
    but if it is not available, they read data from a secondary replica.
- `secondary`: Clients read data only from the secondary replicas.
- `secondaryPreferred`: Clients prefer to read data from a secondary replica,
    but if none are available, they read data from the primary replica.
- `nearest`: Clients read data from the replica that responds the fastest,
    regardless of whether it is a primary or secondary replica.
```

The read preference mode affects data consistency because it determines from which replica clients read data. Reading data from a
secondary replica can result in lower consistency because secondary
replicas may lag behind the primary replica, and may not have the
latest version of the data. Reading data from the primary replica
ensures higher consistency because it has the latest version of the
data.

In summary, data consistency in MongoDB can be controlled through
write concern and read preference settings. Higher write concern levels and reading from the primary replica ensure higher consistency,
while lower write concern levels and reading from secondary replicas can result in lower consistency. It is important to choose the
appropriate write concern and read preference settings based on the
application's requirements for data consistency, availability, and performance.

4.10   How do you configure and use Mon-goDB Change Streams to track data changes in real-time?

MongoDB Change Streams allow application developers to monitor
changes to their MongoDB data in real-time. Change Streams can
watch for changes at the individual document level or at the database
or collection level, and they can be configured to send notifications to
applications whenever documents are inserted, modified, or deleted.

To use MongoDB Change Streams, you first need to create a cursor

on a MongoDB collection or database. You can do this by calling the
'watch()' method on the collection object, passing in a query object
that specifies the data changes you want to track. For example, to
track all insertions into a collection, you can call:

```
const cursor = db.collection('mycollection').watch([{ $match: { operationType:
    'insert' } }])
```

Once you have a cursor, you can use it to read pending changes from
the MongoDB server in real-time. The cursor is updated every time
a change is detected, so you can wait for new changes to arrive by
polling the cursor periodically:

```
while (!cursor.isClosed()) {
  if (cursor.hasNext()) {
    const next = cursor.next()
    console.log(next)
  } else {
    sleep(1000)
  }
}
```

Change Stream events are represented as plain JavaScript objects,
containing information about the type of change ('insert', 'update',
'replace', 'delete', 'invalidate'), the database and collection affected
by the change, and the specific document(s) that were changed. For
example:

```
{
  "_id": {
    "_data": "825FAD8D53...C57E8915023",
    "operationType": "insert"
  },
  "fullDocument": {
    "_id": "5c003155abf51d0fd7b23d72",
    "name": "Alice",
    "age": 30
  },
  "ns": {
    "db": "mydatabase",
    "coll": "mycollection"
  },
  "documentKey": {
    "_id": "5c003155abf51d0fd7b23d72"
  }
}
```

Change Streams can also be customized to include additional filtering,
sorting, or aggregation operations before they are read by the client.
For example:

```
const pipeline = [
```

```
    { $match: { operationType: 'insert', 'fullDocument.age': { $gt: 20 } } },
    { $sort: { 'fullDocument.age': -1 } },
    { $group: { _id: null, count: { $sum: 1 } } }
]

const options = {
  fullDocument: 'updateLookup',
  startAtOperationTime: new Timestamp(0, Date.now() / 1000),
  batchSize: 100
}

const cursor = db.collection('mycollection').watch(pipeline, options)
```

Here, we are watching for 'insert' operations where the 'age' field of
the new document is greater than '20'. We are then sorting the resulting documents by age in descending order and aggregating them into
a single document that contains a count of the number of matching
documents.

Overall, MongoDB Change Streams offer a powerful and flexible tool
for monitoring live data changes in MongoDB. By configuring and using Change Streams effectively, developers can build applications that
respond to data changes in real-time, improving their responsiveness
and utility for end-users.

4.11 What are the differences between the MongoDB Atlas managed service and self-hosted MongoDB deployments?

MongoDB can be deployed in two ways: using MongoDB Atlas, which
is a cloud-based fully managed version of MongoDb, or self-hosted
deployments, which give organizations greater control over the configuration and configuration of the system.

MongoDB Atlas is a cloud-based service that allows organizations
to quickly and easily deploy, scale, and manage MongoDB clusters.
This service eliminates the need for dedicated hardware and reduces
operational overhead by allowing organizations to focus on their applications and data, rather than infrastructure maintenance.

On the other hand, self-hosted deployments give organizations greater
control over the configurations and configurations of the MongoDB
databases they host. Self-hosted deployments can be implemented on

any infrastructure, including on-premise, cloud-based or hybrid environments, depending on the needs of the organization. Self-hosted deployments are ideal for organizations that require more control over their databases, need custom configurations or for organizations that cannot use a cloud-based managed service for compliance or security reasons.

Some differences between the two include the following:

1. Setup and Configuration: With MongoDB Atlas, setup and configuration is quick and easy as most of the setup process is automated. Self-hosted systems, on the other hand, require more manual configurations, which can be more involving.

2. Scalability: MongoDB Atlas scales easily and automatically with features like auto-scaling and sharding. Self-hosted systems require manual scaling and configuration, which can be a challenge for organizations with limited resources.

3. Security: MongoDB Atlas provides built-in security features, such as authentication and authorization, encryption at rest and in transit, and network security configurations. Self-hosted systems require manual configuration of the security features and open up additional attack surfaces that might not be present in the MongoDB Atlas service.

4. Cost: MongoDB Atlas, like other cloud-based offerings, is subscription-based and has a monthly cost, while self-hosted deployments cost more in terms of hardware, maintenance, and the time of the staff members that take care of it. However, costs associated with self-hosted deployments come with the added benefit of greater control and customizability.

In summary, MongoDB Atlas is a great option for organizations that need to deploy quickly and easily and are willing to pay a monthly fee for the convenience. However, self-hosted deployments are the best option for organizations that need greater control and customization of the MongoDB databases they host, although they require more technical know-how and maintenance to operate them.

4.12 Describe the process of setting up and configuring a MongoDB replica set for high availability.

A MongoDB replica set is a group of MongoDB servers that maintain the same data set, providing redundancy and high availability. Setting up and configuring a replica set involves the following steps:

1. Install MongoDB: The first step is to install MongoDB on each server that will be a member of the replica set. The installation process will vary depending on the operating system and distribution.

2. Configure the MongoDB instances: Once MongoDB is installed, each instance needs to be configured with a unique hostname or IP address, and a common replica set name. This can be done by editing the mongod.conf configuration file, which is typically located in the /etc/mongodb/ directory on Linux systems.

3. Initialize the replica set: To initialize the replica set, choose one of the MongoDB instances to be the primary member, and then connect to it using the mongo shell. Use the rs.initiate() function to create a new replica set, specifying the hostname or IP address of each member, along with their corresponding port numbers. For example, the following command can be used to initialize a three-member replica set with members listening on ports 27017, 27018, and 27019:

```
> rs.initiate( {
   _id : "myreplica",
   members: [
     { _id: 0, host: "mongo1.example.net:27017" },
     { _id: 1, host: "mongo2.example.net:27018" },
     { _id: 2, host: "mongo3.example.net:27019" }
   ]
})
```

4. Add members to the replica set: After the replica set is initialized, additional members can be added to it using the rs.add() function. This function requires the hostname or IP address of the new member, along with its corresponding port number. For example, the following command can be used to add a new member listening on port 27020:

```
> rs.add("mongo4.example.net:27020")
```

5. Monitor the replica set: Finally, it is important to monitor the health and status of the replica set to ensure that it is providing high availability and redundancy. This can be done using the rs.status() function and the MongoDB log files.

In summary, setting up and configuring a MongoDB replica set for high availability involves installing MongoDB on each server, configuring the MongoDB instances, initializing the replica set, adding members to the replica set, and monitoring the replica set for health and status.

4.13   How do you monitor and manage slow queries in MongoDB?

Monitoring and managing slow queries in MongoDB is crucial for ensuring good performance and optimizing your database. Here are several ways to do it:

1) Use MongoDB's built-in profiler:
MongoDB has a built-in profiler that logs information on slow operations. The profiler can be configured to log information on slow queries, commands, and database operations. The profiler data can be used to identify slow queries and optimize them. There are three profiling modes:

- Off (0): profiling is disabled.

- Slow Op (1): profiles operations slower than specified query execution time in milliseconds (by default 100ms).

- All Op (2): profiles all operations.

To enable profiling, set the profiling level to either 1 or 2 for a specific database using the following command:

```
db.setProfilingLevel(1, { slowms: 100 })
```

This command sets the profiling level to Slow Op and logs queries that take more than 100 milliseconds to execute.

To view the profiling data, use the following command:

```
db.system.profile.find().pretty()
```

2) Use MongoDB Compass:
MongoDB Compass is a graphical user interface for MongoDB that can be used to monitor and manage slow queries. Compass has a built-in performance analysis tool that provides visibility into query and index usage metrics. It can help you identify slow queries and optimize them easily by providing an easy-to-use UI.

To access this tool, click on the 'Performance' tab and select the desired database and collection. This will bring up a dashboard that shows useful metrics such as slow queries, index usage, and query patterns.

3) Use third-party tools:
Several third-party monitoring and management tools are available for MongoDB that can help with monitoring slow queries. Some popular options include:

- MMS (MongoDB Management Service): a cloud-based monitoring tool provided by MongoDB Inc.

- Ops Manager: an on-premise monitoring and management tool provided by MongoDB Inc.

- Datadog: a third-party monitoring tool that provides integration with MongoDB.

In conclusion, monitoring and managing slow queries in MongoDB is important to maintain database performance. Using the built-in profiler, MongoDB Compass or third-party tools, you can easily identify slow queries and optimize them for better performance.

4.14   Explain the concept of oplog (operation log) in MongoDB replica sets, and why is it important?

In MongoDB, a replica set is a group of mongod processes that maintain the same data set, providing high availability and redundancy. Within a replica set, there is one primary node that receives all write operations and updates the data set. The other nodes in the replica set are secondary nodes that replicate the operations performed by the primary node to maintain the same data set.

To replicate the operations from the primary node to the secondary nodes in the replica set, MongoDB uses oplog (short for operation log), which is a collection of documents that contain a record of all write operations made to the primary node. The oplog is a capped collection that works as a buffer and has a fixed size, meaning that it can store only a limited number of documents, and once the limit is reached, the oldest documents are removed to make room for new ones.

The primary node writes every operation that modifies the data set to the oplog in a format that can be read and replicated by the secondary nodes. The secondary nodes read the oplog and apply the operations to their copies of the data to keep their data sets in sync with the primary node. The oplog ensures that all the operations are performed on all the nodes in the replica set, in the same order they were performed on the primary node. This way, if the primary node fails, one of the secondary nodes can be promoted to primary and continue processing new write operations.

The oplog is essential for the durability and consistency of the data set in a replica set. Without the oplog, there would be no way for the secondary nodes to know what changes were made to the data set, and they would not be able to synchronize their copies. The oplog also allows for failover, which is the process of promoting a secondary node to primary in case the primary node fails or becomes unavailable.

Here is an example of how the oplog works. Suppose we have a replica set with three nodes, A (primary), B, and C (secondary). Suppose also that a new document "x" is inserted into a collection "coll" on the primary node A. The oplog entry for this operation might look like this:

```
{
  "ts": Timestamp(1626349723, 1),
  "op": "i",
  "ns": "test.coll",
  "o": { "_id": ObjectId("60ecf63df9255b5db5d5fd30"), "name": "x" }
}
```

In this example, "ts" represents the timestamp of the operation, "op" represents the operation type (in this case, "i" for insert), "ns" represents the namespace of the collection, and "o" represents the actual operation content (the new document inserted).

The secondary nodes B and C will read this oplog entry and apply it to their copy of the data set, inserting the document "x" into their copies of the "coll" collection. This way, all nodes in the replica set keep the same data set.

In summary, the oplog is crucial for maintaining a consistent data set in a MongoDB replica set. It ensures that all nodes in the replica set have the same data and can survive node failures.

4.15   What are the different types of MongoDB cursors, and how do they affect query performance?

MongoDB offers three types of cursors – Basic, Cursor Snapshot and Tailable. Each of these cursors have their own unique characteristics and affect the query performance in different ways.

1. Basic Cursor: Basic cursor represents the default behavior of the MongoDB query. In a basic cursor, the client issues a query to the server and the database returns the results to client in batches. The size of each batch is determined by the server, and it's default value is 101 records.

To retrieve data from the basic cursor, we use the 'findOne()' or 'next()' method on the cursor. However, if the result set is very large, it may cause performance issues as it can potentially fill up the memory of the application.

2. Cursor Snapshot: When we have to iterate over a large collection and the data inside it is being modified by another process, we should use a Snapshot Cursor to avoid performance issues caused by collection size or modification. A Snapshot Cursor returns the data on the server, as it exists at the start of the query, and that data remains static.

A Snapshot Cursor disables the database from updating the data
returned by the cursor. This is useful when we need to make queries
on a collection without allowing any changes to the collection until
the query is completed.

Consider the following example where we want a static result set for
an inventory collection:

```
const inventory = db.inventory.find({})
const snapshotCursor = inventory.snapshot()

snapshotCursor.forEach(printjson)
```

3. Tailable Cursor: Tailable Cursor is a special type of cursor that
keeps on fetching data from a collection even after the client has ex-
hausted the initial results set. This type of cursor is used to maintain
a stream of information.

A tailable cursor is used when we want to create a capped collection,
which has limited size and always returns the items in the order in
which they were inserted. It continues to return data to the client as
it's inserted by other clients or processes.

Tailable Cursors also allows us to use server side listeners to affect
application behavior when the cursors insert new documents. This is
useful when we want to stream documents in real-time to an application without polling the database incessantly.

Consider the following example where we insert documents into a
capped collection and read them:

```
db.createCollection("my_collection", {capped: true, size: 1000, max: 3})

db.my_collection.insert({"name": "document1"})
db.my_collection.insert({"name": "document2"})
db.my_collection.insert({"name": "document3"})

const cursor = db.my_collection.find().sort({$natural: 1}).tailable(true)

while(cursor.hasNext()){
  let doc = cursor.next()
  printjson(doc)
  sleep(1000)
}
```

In conclusion, Basic Cursor are ideal for small collections whereas
Snapshot and Tailable Cursors are useful for optimizing specific use
cases. Through proper evaluation of requirements and using the right
cursor type, we can ensure the optimised use of resources and im-

proved query execution time.

4.16   How can you use the $expr operator in MongoDB to perform complex queries with aggregation expressions?

The '$expr' operator is used in MongoDB to perform complex queries using aggregation expressions. With this operator, you can use any aggregation expression in the query, including arithmetic operations, boolean logic, and string manipulation. The main benefits of using '$expr' operator are that it allows you to filter documents based on complex criteria that cannot be expressed in a simple query and it runs using the aggregation pipeline, which provides a flexible and powerful way to query MongoDB.

Let us consider an example to understand how we can use the '$expr' operator. Suppose we have a collection 'sales' that contains documents with the following fields: 'product', 'quantity', and 'price'. We want to find all products that have sold for a total revenue of more than $1000. We can use the following aggregation query with the '$expr' operator to achieve this:

```
db.sales.aggregate([
  {
    $group: {
      _id: "$product",
      totalRevenue: { $sum: { $multiply: [ "$quantity", "$price" ] } }
    }
  },
  {
    $match: {
      $expr: { $gt: [ "$totalRevenue", 1000 ] }
    }
  }
])
```

In this query, we first group the documents by 'product' and calculate the total revenue for each product using the '$sum' and '$multiply' operators in the projection stage. Then we use the '$expr' operator to match only those documents where the calculated 'totalRevenue' is greater than '1000'.

The '$expr' operator can also be used to perform more complex

queries using other aggregation expressions. For example, suppose
we want to find all documents in a collection 'orders' where the quantity is less than the average quantity for all orders. We can use the
following aggregation query with the '$expr' operator to achieve this:

```
db.orders.aggregate([
  {
    $group: {
      _id: null,
      avgQuantity: { $avg: "$quantity" }
    }
  },
  {
    $match: {
      $expr: { $gt: [ "$quantity", "$avgQuantity" ] }
    }
  }
])
```

In this query, we first use the '$avg' operator to calculate the av-
erage quantity for all orders. Then we use the '$expr' operator to
match only those documents where the 'quantity' is greater than the
'avgQuantity' calculated in the previous stage.

In conclusion, the '$expr' operator in MongoDB is a powerful tool
that allows you to filter documents based on complex criteria using
aggregation expressions. By using the '$expr' operator in the aggre-
gation pipeline, you can easily perform complex queries that cannot
be expressed in a simple query.

4.17   Describe the process of setting up and configuring a MongoDB sharded cluster for horizontal scaling.

Setting up and configuring a MongoDB sharded cluster for horizontal
scaling is a complex process, but it can greatly improve the performance and scalability of a MongoDB database. Here are the general
steps involved in setting up and configuring a MongoDB sharded cluster:

1. Plan the Cluster:

The first step in setting up a sharded cluster is to plan the overall architecture of the cluster. This includes deciding how many shard servers to use, what type of hardware they will run on, and how many replica sets will be needed. You also need to plan the distribution of data across the cluster to ensure optimal performance.

2. Install MongoDB:

Next, you need to install MongoDB on each server in the cluster. This includes both the mongod and mongos processes. You should also configure the environment variables and system settings on each server to optimize performance.

3. Configure Replica Sets:

Before setting up the sharded cluster, you need to configure replica sets on each shard server. This will help ensure high availability in case of server failures. You should also configure the priority and voting settings of each replica set member.

4. Configure the Config Servers:

The config servers are a critical component of the sharded cluster, as they store the cluster metadata that governs how data is distributed across the shards. You should install and configure the config servers on separate servers from the shard servers to ensure high availability.

5. Start the Sharded Cluster:

Once you have configured the replica sets and config servers, you can start the mongos process on each application server that will access the sharded cluster. The mongos process acts as a router for client requests and routes queries to the appropriate shard server.

6. Add Shards to the Cluster:

Next, you need to add the shard servers to the sharded cluster. This involves connecting to each shard server with the mongos process and issuing the addShard command. You also need to configure the chunk size for each shard to determine how data is distributed across the cluster.

7. Test and Monitor the Cluster:

Finally, you should test the sharded cluster to ensure it is working correctly and monitor it to identify and resolve any issues that arise. You can use various monitoring tools to track the performance and health of the cluster as it scales horizontally.

Here is an example of configuring a sharded cluster of three replica sets across two shards on a local environment:

1. Plan the Cluster:

We have two nodes available in the local environment, which will be used to host the MongoDB shards.

2. Install MongoDB:

On each node, we install MongoDB community edition from the official repository.

3. Configure Replica Sets:

On each node, we configure a replica set with three members:

```
mongod --replSet rs0 --port 27017 --dbpath /data/1 --bind_ip 192.168.1.1

mongod --replSet rs0 --port 27018 --dbpath /data/1 --bind_ip 192.168.1.1

mongod --replSet rs0 --port 27019 --dbpath /data/1 --bind_ip 192.168.1.1
```

4. Configure the Config Servers:

On the third node, we configure three config servers:

```
mongod --configsvr --replSet configs --port 27017 --dbpath /data/1 --bind_ip
    192.168.1.3

mongod --configsvr --replSet configs --port 27018 --dbpath /data/1 --bind_ip
    192.168.1.3

mongod --configsvr --replSet configs --port 27019 --dbpath /data/1 --bind_ip
    192.168.1.3
```

5. Start the Sharded Cluster:

On each application server, we start the mongos process:

```
mongos --configdb configs
    /192.168.1.3:27017,192.168.1.3:27018,192.168.1.3:27019
```

6. Add Shards to the Cluster:

From the mongos process, we add both shards to the cluster:

```
sh.addShard("rs0/192.168.1.1:27017,192.168.1.1:27018,192.168.1.1:27019")
sh.addShard("rs0/192.168.1.2:27017,192.168.1.2:27018,192.168.1.2:27019")
```

7. Test and Monitor the Cluster:

We can now test the sharded cluster by running queries against the mongos process and monitoring the performance of the cluster with tools like MongoDB Compass or the Mongo shell command db.server-Status().

4.18   How do you manage backups in Mon-goDB, and what are the different backup strategies available?

Backup management in MongoDB is a crucial task that ensures safety and recovery against potential data loss resulting from hardware failure, software bugs, or human error. MongoDB provides multiple backup strategies, which can be used in a planned and organized fashion based on the requirements, resources, and complexity of the deployment.

The following are the different backup strategies available in Mon-goDB:

1. Mongodump and Mongorestore:
Mongodump is a straightforward and straightforward tool provided by MongoDB to backup MongoDB data by dumping the data into BSON format in a specified directory. In contrast, Mongorestore restores the data from the BSON dump files into the MongoDB instance. One key advantage of this strategy is that it provides a flexible and straightforward way of restoring specific databases or collections from the backups. However, Mongodump and Mongorestore are not recommended for a large-scale database deployment as they can result in extensive usage of memory and CPU.

Example of using mongodump to backup a collection:

```
mongodump --db mydb --collection mycollection --out /backup/dump/
```

2. AWS S3 and other cloud services:
Many cloud service providers, such as AWS S3, offer cloud storage for
backing up MongoDB data. These services provide a secure and scalable platform to store and retrieve data backups, which can be used
for disaster recovery and data migration. The backup operations can
be automated using scripts, and the deployment can be customized
based on availability and reliability requirements.

Example of using AWS S3 to backup a database:

```
mongodump --archive --gzip --db mydb | aws s3 cp - s3://mybucket/mydb.dmp.gz
```

3. MongoDB Backup Service:
MongoDB provides a cloud-based backup service that is specifically
built for backing up MongoDB data. The MongoDB Backup Service is
a fully managed service that provides automated, continuous backups
of your data, with near-zero RPO (Recovery Point Objective) and
RTO (Recovery Time Objective) targets. It provides enterprise-grade
data protection, monitoring, and support, and can be used for any
deployment, whether on-premise or cloud-based.

Example of backing up data using MongoDB Backup Service:

```
mongodump --uri="mongodb+srv://<username>:<password>@<clustername>.mongodb.
    net/test" --gzip --archive | mongobackup upload --username=<accessKey>
    --password=<secretKey> --bucket=my-bucket --file=test.gz
```

4. File System Snapshots:
File system snapshots are disk-based backups that capture the entire
image of the server's file system, including MongoDB's data files.
This is a low-overhead method for creating point-in-time backups of
database systems. This method is ideal for very large databases where
backups can take a long time and impact availability significantly.

Example of creating a file system snapshot(using LVM) for backup:

```
umount /mnt/data
lvcreate --size 100G --snapshot --name snap-lvm /dev/vg_data/lv_data
mount /dev/vg_data/snap-lvm /mnt/data_snapshot
tar -czvf data_snapshot.tar.gz /mnt/data_snapshot
```

In conclusion, it is essential to choose the backup strategy based
on the deployment's complexity, scale, and availability requirements.
Proper backup management will ensure data is recoverable, and the
organization can get back to normal operations quickly in case of a

disaster.

4.19 What is a MongoDB zone sharding, and how does it improve data distribution and query performance?

MongoDB zone sharding allows you to specify data partitioning based on a specific range of values for a field in a collection, called the sharding key. This can improve data distribution and query performance by ensuring that data is evenly distributed across the nodes in a sharded cluster and by allowing queries that use the sharding key to target a specific range of data within a collection.

In MongoDB, sharding is the process of storing data across multiple servers, called shards, in order to improve scalability and performance. With zone sharding, you can define partitions, or zones, within each shard based on the values of a sharding key. The goal of zone sharding is to ensure that each zone contains roughly the same amount of data, which allows for more efficient query routing and faster query times.

For example, suppose you have a collection of customer data with a sharding key of 'zip_code'. You can define partitions or zones based on ranges of zip codes, such as 00000-49999, 50000-99999, and so on. In this case, each zone will contain customers from a specific range of zip codes. As new customers are added to the collection, MongoDB will automatically balance the data across the zones to ensure even distribution.

Using zone sharding can also improve query performance by allowing you to target a specific range of data within a collection. When a query includes the sharding key, MongoDB can route the query to the appropriate zone, which can significantly reduce the amount of data that needs to be scanned. This can be particularly useful for range queries, which can be expensive when executed across a large collection.

In addition to improving data distribution and query performance, zone sharding can also help you optimize your sharded cluster for

different types of workloads. For example, if you have a collection of
time-series data, you can use a sharding key based on the timestamp
to ensure that data is evenly distributed across different time periods.
Similarly, if you have a collection of geospatial data, you can use
a sharding key based on the location to ensure that data is evenly
distributed across different geographic regions.

Overall, MongoDB zone sharding is a powerful tool for managing large
amounts of data in a sharded cluster. By defining partitions based on
a sharding key, you can ensure even data distribution, faster query
performance, and better scalability for your MongoDB deployment.

4.20   Explain the role of the aggregation pipeline in MongoDB's BI (Business Intelligence) Connector.

MongoDB's BI Connector is a powerful tool that enables users to
perform SQL queries on MongoDB data using traditional BI (Business Intelligence) tools such as Tableau, Qlik, and Microsoft Excel.
However, the structure of MongoDB documents does not always fit
well with the tabular structure that BI tools expect.

This is where the aggregation pipeline comes in - it allows users to
shape and format the data in MongoDB to meet the needs of the BI
tool. The aggregation pipeline is a framework for performing complex data transformation and analysis operations on MongoDB documents. It includes a set of stages that can be used to filter, group,
sort, and aggregate data in a flexible and powerful way.

For example, let's say we have a collection of customers with the
following structure:

```
{
    _id: ObjectId("5fca48d94108d6a3a66e464a"),
    name: "John␣Smith",
    age: 35,
    gender: "male",
    address: {
        street: "123␣Main␣St",
        city: "Anytown",
        state: "CA",
        zip: "12345"
    },
```

```
    purchases: [
      { product: "Shoes", price: 50 },
      { product: "Shirt", price: 25 },
      { product: "Pants", price: 40 }
    ]
}
```

To use this data in a BI tool, we may want to aggregate the total price of all purchases for each customer, as well as the total revenue for the entire collection. We can accomplish this with the following aggregation pipeline stages:

```
[
  {
    $unwind: "$purchases"
  },
  {
    $group: {
      _id: "$_id",
      name: { $first: "$name" },
      total: { $sum: "$purchases.price" }
    }
  },
  {
    $group: {
      _id: null,
      totalRevenue: { $sum: "$total" },
      customers: { $push: "$$ROOT" }
    }
  }
]
```

Let's break down what's happening in each stage:

1. '$unwind': This stage "flattens" the 'purchases' array, creating a separate document for each purchase. Our example document would now become three separate documents, each with a different 'purchases' object.

2. '$group': This stage groups the documents by '_id' (which is the same for each document since we haven't done anything to change it). We also use the '$first' operator to ensure that the 'name' field is available to us in the next stage. Finally, we use the '$sum' operator to add up the 'price' field for each purchase within the group.

3. '$group': This stage groups all of the documents from the previous stage together into a single document with '_id' set to 'null'. We use the '$sum' operator again to calculate the total revenue for the entire collection. We also use the '$push' operator to create an array of the customers, each with their own 'total' field calculated in the previous

stage.

The result of this aggregation pipeline would be a single document with the following structure:

```
{
  _id: null,
  totalRevenue: 115,
  customers: [
    { _id: ObjectId("5fca48d94108d6a3a66e464a"), name: "John Smith", total:
       115 }
  ]
}
```

This document can now be queried by a BI tool using standard SQL syntax. We can connect Tableau to MongoDB using the BI Connector and write a query like this:

```
SELECT name, total FROM mydb.customers
```

The result would be a simple table with the name and total for each customer, ready to be visualized in Tableau or any other BI tool.

In summary, the aggregation pipeline plays a critical role in shaping MongoDB data for use in BI tools. Its flexible, modular structure allows for complex data transformation and analysis operations that can be tailored to meet the specific needs of the user.

Chapter 5

Expert

5.1 What are the differences between the various MongoDB consistency models (strong, eventual, and session)?

MongoDB supports three types of consistency models: Strong consistency, Eventual consistency and Session consistency.

Strong Consistency (Default): In MongoDB, strong consistency refers to the guarantee that a read operation always returns the most recently written data on the primary node. In other words, strong consistency ensures that a write operation is propagated to all nodes before a read operation is processed. When a write operation is performed, it is acknowledged immediately only after the data is replicated to a majority of nodes within the cluster. In other words, an acknowledged write operation guarantees that the write operation applied to a majority of nodes within the cluster. Thus, when a read operation is performed, MongoDB verifies the latest data across all nodes and returns it. Strong consistency provides intra-document consistency; this means that if two fields are updated in one document, the fields will be consistent across all reads.

An example of how strong consistency works is when a write operation

1 updates the value of a field F in a document. The write operation is an acknowledged write operation, indicating that the write operation applied to a majority of the cluster. After this, a read operation for the same document will always return the most recently written data with the updated value of field F.

Eventual Consistency: In MongoDB, eventual consistency refers to a consistency model that provides weak guarantees of the order in which write operations will be visible. Write operations are applied immediately to the node where the write operation occurred. However, this write operation is eventually propagated to all other nodes in the cluster asynchronously.

In other words, eventual consistency allows some delay in the replication of data between nodes where read operations can receive stale data. Distributed systems using eventual consistency can handle node disconnection or network disruptions to certain nodes without causing extended periods of system inaccessibility.

An example of how eventual consistency works is when write operations 1 and 2 are performed on a document, and the read operation occurs between these writes. The possible results can be read 1 (before write 1), read 2 (after write 1 but before write 2) or read 3 (after write 2).

Session Consistency: Session consistency is a MongoDB consistency model that provides a balance between strong and eventual consistency. This consistency model maintains consistency within the session between a client and a single node using read-your-writes guarantees. In other words, this consistency model guarantees that any read operation performed within a session sees the results of all previous write operations within the same session, providing stronger consistency guarantees than eventual consistency.

An example of how session consistency works is when a client application initiates a session to a node, write operations 1 and 2 are performed on the document, and the read operation occurs between these writes within the same session. The only possible result will be read 2 (after write 2). Any subsequent operations executed within the same session will read the updated value.

In summary, MongoDB offers three types of consistency models: strong,

eventual, and session consistency. Strong consistency guarantees that read operations always return the most recently written data, while eventual consistency provides weaker guarantees but allows for some delay in replication. Session consistency provides a balance between strong and eventual consistency by maintaining consistency within a session between a client and a single node using read-your-writes guarantees.

5.2   How do you handle complex data migrations in MongoDB while maintaining data consistency and minimizing downtime?

Handling complex data migrations in MongoDB can be challenging, especially when the data involved is critical to business operations. To maintain data consistency and minimize downtime, there are a few strategies you can use:

1. Develop a migration plan:
Before embarking on any major data migration, it is critical to have a well-defined migration plan to guide the process. The migration plan should identify:

- The source and target databases

- The data to be migrated

- The order in which the data will be migrated

- Any necessary transformations or conversions

- How the migration will be tested and validated

A migration plan helps minimize the risk of data loss, consistency issues, and downtime during the migration process.

2. Use replica sets:
Replica sets allow you to migrate data with minimal downtime. By setting up a secondary replica set, you can migrate data to the secondary server in the background while the primary server remains available. Once the migration is complete, you can switch the pri-

mary server to the new replica set and begin serving data from the
new server.

3. Use sharding:
Sharding enables you to migrate large amounts of data while maintaining availability and consistency. By dividing the data across multiple shards, you can migrate each shard independently without af-
fecting the availability of the rest of the database.

4. Use the MongoDB Connector for BI:
The MongoDB Connector for BI allows you to migrate data directly
from MongoDB to your preferred data warehousing platform, such
as Amazon Redshift, Google BigQuery, or Apache Spark. With the
connector, you can migrate data to a new environment without the
need for complex ETL processes.

5. Use batch processing:
If you need to migrate a significant amount of data, batch processing
can help you manage the data migration. By breaking the migration
process into smaller, manageable batches, you can minimize downtime
and reduce the risk of data loss or consistency issues.

In summary, handling complex data migrations in MongoDB while
maintaining data consistency and minimizing downtime requires careful planning and execution. By using replica sets, sharding, the MongoDB Connector for BI, and batch processing, you can migrate your
data with confidence and minimal disruption to your business operations.

5.3   Explain the impact of different write concern settings on the performance and durability of MongoDB operations.

In MongoDB, write concern determines how many replicas of a write
operation must confirm the write before it is considered successful.
Write concern specified at the client level or at the configuration level
for each instance can impact performance and durability of MongoDB
operations.

There are several write concern levels available in MongoDB:

- 'w: 0' - The write operation does not wait for the server to confirm the write operation.

- 'w: 1' - The write operation waits for the primary replica to confirm the write operation.

- 'w: "majority"' - The write operation waits for a majority of the replicas to confirm the write operation.

- 'w: "<number>"' - The write operation waits for the specified number of replicas to confirm the write operation.

- 'w: "tagSetName"' - The write operation waits for the tagged set (set of replicas matching the specified tag set) to confirm the write operation.

Higher write concerns can improve the durability of write operations, but it usually comes at the cost of performance. Setting a higher write concern level means that MongoDB waits longer for confirmation of the write operation, which leads to increased latency. In contrast, lower write concern levels like 'w: 0' can improve performance by allowing operations to complete more quickly, but there is a higher risk of data loss if an error occurs before the write can be replicated.

For example, if you have a MongoDB cluster with three nodes and you set the write concern to 'w: "majority"', the write operation must be confirmed by at least two of the replicas. This ensures that even if one node fails, the write operation is still available in a majority of the nodes. However, this level of durability comes at the cost of increased latency.

On the other hand, if you set the write concern to 'w: 0', the write operation completes as soon as the server accepts the write request. This can offer faster write performance, but it is also riskier as there is no guarantee that the data is written to any replica, increasing the chances of data loss.

Overall, choosing the right write concern level is a trade-off between performance and durability, depending on the needs of the application. It is important to choose the appropriate write concern level based on the specific use case requirements such as the importance of the data being written, the risk of data loss, and the performance requirements.

5.4 Discuss the pros and cons of using multi-document transactions in MongoDB, and when they should be used.

Multi-document transactions in MongoDB allow the user to group multiple operations together and either commit them all at once or roll them all back if any of the operations fail. These transactions can span multiple documents and even multiple collections or databases. While there are certainly advantages to using multi-document transactions, there are also drawbacks that must be taken into consideration.

Pros: 1. Atomic operations: Multi-document transactions guarantee that all operations are completed or none are. This means that if any part of the transaction fails, all changes are rolled back to their previous state, ensuring data consistency.

2. Availability: In previous versions of MongoDB, transactions were only available on replica sets. However, with the release of MongoDB 4.2, transactions are now available in sharded clusters as well, allowing for greater flexibility and scalability.

3. Simplified code logic: By grouping multiple operations together, the code logic can be simplified and the number of database calls can be reduced. This can lead to better performance and reduced complexity.

Cons: 1. Performance: Multi-document transactions may not perform as well as single-document operations, especially for large or complex transactions. Transactions require locking of resources during the transaction, which can cause contention and reduce overall performance. Additionally, transactions are limited to a single replica set or shard, which can also impact performance.

2. Data throughput: Multi-document transactions require more data to be sent between the client and the database. This can reduce data throughput, causing slower response times.

3. Limitations: Multi-document transactions have some limitations, including the inability to perform an operation in multiple shards, and the inability to perform transactions on some types of operations (in-

cluding map-reduce and text search). Additionally, transactions have a limit on the number of documents they can operate on (currently set at 1,000).

When to use multi-document transactions: Multi-document transactions are most commonly used in situations where data consistency is critical, such as financial transactions or other scenarios where incomplete transactions could cause problems. Additionally, they can be used in cases where simplifying code logic or reducing the number of database calls will lead to improved performance. However, it is important to carefully consider the drawbacks and limitations of multi-document transactions before implementing them, and to test for performance and scalability before deploying them in production environments.

Example usage code of transactions in MongoDB:

```
const session = client.startSession();
session.startTransaction();
try {
  const usersCollection = client.db("test").collection("users");
  const accountsCollection = client.db("test").collection("accounts");

  await usersCollection.updateOne(
    { _id: userId },
    { $inc: { balance: amount } },
    { session }
  );

  await accountsCollection.updateOne(
    { _id: accountId },
    { $inc: { balance: -amount } },
    { session }
  );

  await session.commitTransaction();
} catch (error) {
  await session.abortTransaction();
  throw error;
} finally {
  session.endSession();
}
```

In this example code, a session is started to begin a transaction. Two collections, "users" and "accounts," are updated within the same transaction using the 'updateOne' method. If any part of the transaction fails, the entire transaction is rolled back by calling 'abortTransaction()'. If all operations are successful, the transaction is committed, and the changes are saved to the database by calling 'commitTransaction()'. Finally, the session is ended.

5.5   Describe the process of analyzing and optimizing a MongoDB query plan using the explain() method.

Analyzing and optimizing a MongoDB query plan can be done using the explain() method. This method is used to get information about the execution of a query, including the execution plan, execution time, and other important details. The explain() method is a powerful tool that helps you understand how MongoDB is executing your queries, and can help you optimize your queries for better performance.

Here are the general steps to analyze and optimize a MongoDB query using the explain() method:

Step 1: Understand the Collection Schema

The first step in optimizing a MongoDB query is to understand the schema of the collection. You need to know the structure of the documents in the collection, the indexes that exist, and how the data is organized. This information will help you determine the best way to query the data and optimize the query.

Step 2: Write the Query

After you have a good understanding of the collection schema, you can write the query. You should be as specific as possible when writing the query, specifying filters, projection, and sorting options.

Step 3: Call explain()

Next, you need to call the explain() method to get information about the query execution. To call explain(), you can simply add the method to the end of your query:

"' db.collection.find(query).explain() "'

The explain() method returns a document that contains details about the query. The document includes the query plan, execution time, index usage, and other important details.

Step 4: Analyze the Query Plan

The most important piece of information returned by explain() is the query plan. The query plan is a series of stages that MongoDB uses to execute the query. Each stage performs a specific operation, such as filtering documents, sorting documents, or retrieving documents from an index.

You should carefully analyze the query plan to identify inefficiencies or areas for optimization. Look for stages that may be slower than others, or for stages that are returning a large number of documents that are not needed.

Step 5: Optimize the Query

Once you have identified areas for optimization, you can make changes to the query to improve its performance. This may involve adding or modifying indexes, changing the query structure, or changing the query parameters.

For example, if you notice that the query is not using an index, you may need to add an index or modify the query to use an existing index. Alternatively, if you notice that the query is retrieving more documents than needed, you may need to add or modify filters to reduce the number of documents returned.

Step 6: Test the Optimized Query

After you have optimized the query, you should test it to make sure it is working as expected. You can call explain() again to make sure the query plan has changed, and to verify that the changes you made have improved performance.

In conclusion, analyzing and optimizing a MongoDB query plan can be done using the explain() method. This method provides detailed information about the query execution, including the query plan, execution time, and index usage. By carefully analyzing the query plan and making optimizations, you can improve the performance of your queries and make your application more efficient.

5.6 How do you troubleshoot and resolve issues related to index contention in MongoDB?

Index contention occurs in MongoDB when multiple read/write operations are accessing the same index at the same time, causing contention and slowing down the performance of the database. There are several ways to troubleshoot and resolve index contention issues in MongoDB:

1. Monitor database performance: Monitoring the database performance using MongoDB monitoring tools like Ops Manager or Performance Advisor can help identify index contention issues. These tools can help identify slow queries, high lock percentages, and other performance issues that could be related to index contention.

2. Analyze index usage: Analyze the usage of indexes in MongoDB to identify which indexes are causing contention issues. Use the explain() method to analyze query execution plans and identify which indexes are being used for each query. Also, use the system.profile collection to track slow queries and analyze which indexes are being used by those queries.

3. Optimize the indexes: Optimize the indexes in MongoDB by removing redundant or unused indexes, creating compound indexes, and using partial indexes. Redundant indexes can be removed to reduce the number of indexes being used by the database. Compound indexes can be created to reduce the number of indexes being used by the database for a specific query. Partial indexes can be used to create indexes on a subset of the documents in a collection.

4. Adjust the read/write ratios: Adjust the read/write ratios in the database to reduce the number of read/write operations happening at the same time. This can be accomplished by using read replicas for read-heavy workloads, or by sharding the data across multiple nodes for write-heavy workloads.

5. Use capped collections: Use capped collections in MongoDB to limit the amount of data being indexed. Capped collections are fixed-size collections that automatically discard old data as new data is added, making them ideal for logging and other similar use cases.

6. Use proper index types: Use the proper index types in MongoDB to avoid index contention issues. For example, unique indexes should only be used when necessary, as they can cause issues with write scalability due to the need for locking.

By following these techniques, MongoDB users can troubleshoot and resolve issues related to index contention and improve the database's overall performance.

5.7 Explain the concept of geospatial indexing in MongoDB, and how it can be used to perform location-based queries.

Geospatial indexing in MongoDB is a feature that allows for the indexing of data based on geospatial information, such as latitude and longitude coordinates. This type of indexing makes it possible for developers to efficiently perform location-based queries on large datasets.

In MongoDB, geospatial indexing is achieved through the use of a special type of index called a geospatial index. To create a geospatial index, developers must specify which field(s) in their documents contain geospatial data. Once this index has been created, queries against the database can make use of it to perform various types of geospatial operations, such as finding all documents within a certain distance from a given point, or finding all documents that intersect with a given geospatial shape.

One common use case for geospatial indexing in MongoDB is in the development of location-based applications. For example, an app that helps users find the nearest restaurant, gas station, or hospital would require access to a database of geospatial information. By using a geospatial index, developers can perform fast and efficient queries to find the closest matches to a given location.

Consider the following example. Suppose we have a collection of documents representing retail stores, each of which includes a name, address, and location field:

```
{
    "name": "Walmart",
    "address": "123 Main St",
    "location": {
        "type": "Point",
        "coordinates": [-122.416943, 37.7749]
    }
}
```

To enable efficient querying based on the 'location' field, we can create a geospatial index like so:

```
db.stores.createIndex({ location: "2dsphere" })
```

This will create a geospatial index for the 'location' field using the '2dsphere' method, which supports querying based on spherical coordinates (i.e. latitude and longitude).

With this index in place, we can perform a wide range of location-based queries on the 'stores' collection. For example, to find all stores within a certain distance of a given point, we can use the '$nearSphere' operator:

```
db.stores.find({
    location: {
        $nearSphere: {
            $geometry: {
                type: "Point",
                coordinates: [-122.41669, 37.78581]
            },
            $maxDistance: 500
        }
    }
})
```

This query will find all stores within 500 meters of the point (-122.41669, 37.78581).

Overall, geospatial indexing in MongoDB is a powerful tool for working with location-based data. By leveraging the geospatial index, developers can quickly and efficiently perform complex queries, making it easier to build high-performance location-based applications.

5.8   How do you use the $graphLookup operator in the MongoDB aggregation framework to perform recursive search on hierarchical data?

The '$graphLookup' operator in the MongoDB aggregation framework can be used to perform recursive search on hierarchical data. This operator searches for documents recursively in a collection or view using the adjacency list model. The operator takes the following parameters:

- 'from': The collection or view to perform the recursive search on.

- 'startWith': The value to start the recursive search with.

- 'connectFromField': The field in the 'from' collection or view that contains the reference to the parent document.

- 'connectToField': The field in the input documents that contains the reference to the child document.

- 'as': The output array field that contains the matching documents.

- 'maxDepth': The maximum recursion depth. If set to a positive integer, the operator will stop the search after that many recursive levels.

- 'restrictSearchWithMatch': An optional query expression that limits the documents processed by the $graphLookup operation.

Here is an example of how to use the '$graphLookup' operator to traverse a tree structure in a collection called 'categories':

```
db.categories.aggregate([
  {
    $graphLookup: {
      from: "categories",
      startWith: "$_id",
      connectFromField: "_id",
      connectToField: "parentId",
      as: "subcategories",
      maxDepth: 5
    }
  }
])
```

In this example, we are traversing a tree structure where each document in the 'categories' collection has a 'parentId' field referencing its parent document. We are starting the search with the '_id' field of the input documents, and creating an output array field called 'sub-categories' that contains all matching documents up to a depth of 5.

The '$graphLookup' operator can return a lot of duplicate documents, especially in cases where circular references exist. To handle this, we can use the '$group' stage to remove duplicates, like this:

```
db.categories.aggregate([
  {
    $graphLookup: {
      from: "categories",
      startWith: "$_id",
      connectFromField: "_id",
      connectToField: "parentId",
      as: "subcategories",
      maxDepth: 5
    }
  },
  {
    $unwind: "$subcategories"
  },
  {
    $group: {
      _id: "$subcategories._id",
      name: { $first: "$subcategories.name" },
      parentId: { $first: "$subcategories.parentId" },
      // any other fields you want to include
    }
  },
  {
    $group: {
      _id: "$_id",
      name: { $first: "$name" },
      parentId: { $first: "$parentId" },
      subcategories: { $push: "$$ROOT" },
    }
  }
])
```

In this example, we first use the '$graphLookup' operator to create an array of subcategories for each input document. Then, we use the '$unwind' stage to flatten the 'subcategories' array. We group the flattened documents by '_id', taking the first value of the 'name' and 'parentId' fields (since they should be the same for all documents with the same '_id'). Finally, we group the documents by '_id' again, creating an array of 'subcategories' for each document.

Overall, the '$graphLookup' operator can be a powerful tool for performing recursive searches on hierarchical data in MongoDB. However, it can be complex to use and can have performance issues if used improperly. It is important to carefully consider your use case and data model before using this operator.

5.9 Discuss the challenges and best practices associated with schema design and data modeling in MongoDB.

MongoDB is a flexible and dynamic NoSQL database that does not enforce a schema or data model. Instead, it relies on a dynamic schema that allows for flexibility in data storage and retrieval. This flexibility, however, can also result in challenges and best practices related to schema design and data modeling.

Challenges of Schema Design and Data Modeling in MongoDB:

1. Data Integrity MongoDB's dynamic schema can make it challenging to maintain data integrity. Without a predefined schema, it can be difficult to ensure that data is consistent across the document.

2. Query Performance The dynamic schema of MongoDB can lead to inefficient queries, especially if indexes are not correctly designed. Designing indexes can be a challenge because the access patterns for documents are less predictable than in a traditional RDBMS.

3. Scalability Without a well-designed schema, scaling a MongoDB cluster can become challenging. As the database grows, it can be difficult to predict how sharding and replication will impact query performance and scalability.

Best Practices for Schema Design and Data Modeling in MongoDB:

1. Understand the Data Access Patterns To ensure efficient queries and good performance, it is essential to understand the access patterns for the data. It is important to consider how the data will be retrieved, what types of queries will be performed, and how frequently they will be executed.

2. Normalize the Data Avoid nesting large sub-documents and repeated fields within a document. Maintain a normalized data model with distinct collections for each type of data where relationships between entities can be established with linking and referencing.

3. Use Indexing Indexing is essential for achieving good query performance using MongoDB. Use compound indexes wherever possible,

and always consider the queries that will be run against the collection.

4. Plan for Growth Design the schema or data model with scalability in mind. Consider the impact that clustering, sharding, and replication will have on query performance and scalability.

5. Perform Regular Maintenance Regular maintenance is important to keep the database running smoothly. This includes maintaining indexes, removing unused indexes or collections, and monitoring query performance.

In conclusion, MongoDB's dynamic schema can make schema design and data modeling challenging, but with careful consideration of data access patterns, normalization, indexing, scalability, and regular maintenance in mind, it is possible to optimize MongoDB databases for efficient and scalable data storage and retrieval.

5.10 Describe strategies for handling large-scale data growth and optimizing storage usage in MongoDB.

MongoDB is a NoSQL database that allows for flexible data modeling, horizontal scaling, and dynamic schema design. However, like any database, as the amount of data stored in MongoDB grows, the management of the database becomes more challenging. In this answer, we will go over the strategies for handling large-scale data growth and optimizing storage usage in MongoDB.

Sharding

One of the main strategies for handling large-scale data growth in MongoDB is sharding. Sharding is a mechanism to distribute data across multiple servers or nodes in a cluster, each of which can handle a subset of the total workload. With sharding, as the amount of data stored in MongoDB grows, additional nodes can be added to the cluster to distribute the workload across more machines. This results in improved performance, scalability, and reliability.

For example, assume we have a MongoDB cluster with two shards,

each consisting of two nodes, and we add a third shard, as shown
below:

```
Shard 1 (Node 1) -> 25 GB
Shard 1 (Node 2) -> 25 GB
Shard 2 (Node 1) -> 25 GB
Shard 2 (Node 2) -> 25 GB
Shard 3 (Node 1) -> 0 GB
Shard 3 (Node 2) -> 0 GB
```

Before adding the third shard, each of the shards contains 50 GB of
data. After the addition of the third shard, the data is automatically
redistributed across all three shards so that each shard now contains
approximately 33

Compression

Another strategy for handling large-scale data growth and optimizing storage usage in MongoDB is compression. Compression involves
reducing the size of data stored in MongoDB by removing redundant
or unnecessary information. MongoDB natively supports compression for storage, which can reduce the storage requirements for the
database and therefore reduce the cost of hardware and cloud storage.

The WiredTiger storage engine, which is the default storage engine for
MongoDB since version 3.2, supports compression at the collection or
index level. The WiredTiger storage engine uses a combination of different compression algorithms, including Snappy, zlib, and BZIP2, to
determine the best compression algorithm for the data being stored.

In MongoDB, compression can be achieved by enabling compression
on a per-collection or per-index basis. For example, the following
command will enable compression for a collection named "myCollection":

```
db.myCollection.createIndex( { "myField": 1 }, { "compression": { "compressor
    ": "zlib" } } );
```

Indexing

Indexing is another important strategy for optimizing storage usage in
MongoDB. Indexes allow MongoDB to retrieve data more efficiently,
reducing the number of disk reads required to fetch data. This results
in improved query performance and reduced storage requirements.

In MongoDB, an index is a data structure that stores a subset of the data in a collection, ordered by the values of the indexed field. When a query is executed, MongoDB can use the index to quickly locate the documents that match the query criteria, rather than scanning the entire collection.

To optimize storage usage in MongoDB, it is important to identify the fields that are frequently used in queries and create indexes on those fields. For example, suppose we have a collection containing customer data, and we frequently query the collection for customers based on their last name. In that case, we can create an index on the "lastName" field, as shown below:

```
db.customers.createIndex( { "lastName": 1 } )
```

Note that creating too many indexes can also negatively impact performance and increase storage requirements, so it is essential to identify the queries that are most frequently executed and create indexes on only those fields that are frequently used in those queries.

Conclusion

In conclusion, MongoDB is an excellent database for handling large-scale data growth and optimizing storage usage. Sharding, compression, and indexing are some of the strategies that can be used to handle data growth, reduce storage requirements, and improve query performance. By choosing the right strategy and implementing it correctly, MongoDB can continue to scale horizontally while remaining performant and cost-effective.

5.11   How do you set up and manage cross-region replication and disaster recovery in MongoDB?

Setting up and managing cross-region replication and disaster recovery in MongoDB can be achieved by following these general steps:

1. Choose a Replication Strategy:
MongoDB provides different replication strategies such as replica sets, sharding, and global clusters. Each one of these replication strategies

is designed to satisfy different use cases, but in this case cross-region replication and disaster recovery, replica sets strategy should be considered. A replica set consists of a primary node that receives all write operations and one or more secondary nodes that replicate that data from the primary.

2. Select a Cloud Platform:
In order to enable cross-region replication, it is necessary to select a cloud platform that supports it. Some popular options are Amazon Web Services (AWS), Google Cloud Platform (GCP), and Microsoft Azure.

3. Set Up the Primary Node:
The first step is to set up the primary node in one region. Assuming that we are using AWS, we can use an EC2 instance to set up our primary node. The following steps are performed on the primary node:

 - Install MongoDB on the instance

 - Configure the MongoDB instance by editing the mongod configuration file, /etc/mongod.conf

 - Start the MongoDB service.

 - Disable the firewall or open communication ports to allow access to the database.

4. Set Up the Secondary Nodes:
The next step is to set up one or more secondary nodes in another region. These secondary nodes will replicate data from the primary node.

```
 - Create another EC2 instance in your desired region
 - Install MongoDB
 - Configure MongoDB to connect to the primary node by specifying the private
     IP address of the primary node in the configuration file, /etc/mongod.
     conf
 - Start the MongoDB service.
```

5. Secure the Network:
To enable replication and disaster recovery between regions securely, virtual private networks (VPNs) should be used to create secure communication channels between them. This will help us to control the traffic flow between regions and make the transmission of data more secure.

6. Configure Replication:

To configure replication, we need to connect to the primary node and initiate the replication process by running the rs.initiate() command:

```
> rs.initiate()
```

This command initiates the replica set and sets the current node as the primary node. Next, we need to add secondary nodes to the replica set by running the rs.add() command:

```
>rs.add("second-node-ip:port")
```

This command adds the second node into the existing replica set.

7. Disaster Recovery:

In case of a disaster in the primary node, the secondary nodes in the replica set can be promoted to a primary nodes to continue processing requests. To make this happen, we need to connect to one of the secondary nodes and initiate the rs.stepDown() command:

```
> rs.stepDown()
```

This command initiates the election process for a new primary node and promotes one of the secondary nodes to act as the new primary node.

In conclusion, setting up and managing cross-region replication and disaster recovery in MongoDB requires a good understanding of replication strategies, cloud platforms, network security, and disaster recovery techniques. By following the above steps, one can set up and maintain a highly available, disaster-resistant MongoDB database.

5.12   What are the various MongoDB maintenance tasks, and how can they be automated for large-scale deployments?

MongoDB requires regular maintenance to ensure that it's running efficiently and reliably. Some of the maintenance tasks are as follows:

1. Backup: Data backups are important because they provide a

mechanism for recovering data that has been lost due to hardware failure, software bugs, or other errors. MongoDB offers several ways to backup data, including using the mongodump and mongorestore tools, which create BSON files that can be restored to a MongoDB deployment.

2. Indexes: MongoDB uses indexes to improve query performance, and indexes must be maintained to ensure they're up to date. MongoDB provides several built-in options for creating and managing indexes, including compound indexes, text indexes, and geospatial indexes.

3. Compact: MongoDB stores data in chunks, and when data is deleted, the space is not immediately released. This can result in fragmentation within a datafile that can degrade performance. The compact command can be used to release the unused space in a datafile.

4. Repair: MongoDB data files can become corrupted due to hardware errors, software bugs, or other issues. The repairDatabase command can be used to repair a corrupted database.

5. Monitoring: Monitoring the health of a MongoDB deployment is crucial to ensuring its reliability and performance. MongoDB provides several built-in tools for monitoring a deployment, including the mongostat and mongotop utilities.

To automate these tasks for large-scale deployments, MongoDB provides several tools and features, including:

1. MongoDB Ops Manager: Ops Manager is a management tool that automates many of the tasks involved in deploying, scaling, and managing MongoDB. It includes features for automated backups, monitoring, alerts and repair.

2. Automation: MongoDB's automation feature enables you to use software to manage your deployment across multiple machines, allowing you to quickly scale to meet demand or recover from failures.

3. MongoDB Atlas: Atlas is a fully managed cloud database service that provides automatic backups, point-in-time recovery, and automated patches and upgrades.

4. Cron jobs: MongoDB maintenance tasks can be automated using

cron jobs or scheduled tasks. For example, a daily backup can be scheduled using a cron job.

In conclusion, MongoDB maintenance tasks are crucial to ensuring the reliability and performance of a deployment. MongoDB provides several built-in tools and features for automating these tasks for large-scale deployments, including Ops Manager, automation, and Atlas. These tools help simplify and streamline the maintenance process, so you can focus on building your application.

5.13 Discuss the differences between the various MongoDB read preferences (primary, primaryPreferred, secondary, secondaryPreferred, and nearest) and their impact on query performance and consistency.

MongoDB provides several read preferences that can be used to configure how queries are distributed among replica set members. These read preferences control which members a query can read data from and how to balance the read load across the members.

The different read preferences are:

- `primary`: Queries are only routed to the primary node of the replica set. This ensures that the data returned by the query is the current data (like all updates have been applied) and suitable for write operations. The query will not run if the primary cannot be found, which might reduce availability.
- `primaryPreferred`: Queries are first routed to the primary, but if it's not available or the latency is too high, the query is routed to a secondary node. This preference can be useful when the data is likely to be up to date, but some flexibility is still required in case of primary node failures or maintenance.
- `secondary`: Queries are only routed to the secondaries of the replica set. This can be useful for read-heavy workloads and off-loading queries from the primary node, to free it up for write operations. However, queries will be less up to date than those run on a primary, and any data the query relies on that is only available in the primary node will not be visible, causing inconsistent results.
- `secondaryPreferred`: Queries prefer to read from secondary nodes, but still tolerates reading from a primary in case of node unavailability. This preference can be useful for read-heavy workloads, particularly if the primary node is expected to be busy or difficult to reach due to network latency. However, queries may still retrieve inconsistent results if the primary node is missing new data.

```
-␣`nearest`:␣Queries␣are␣routed␣to␣the␣node␣with␣the␣lowest␣network␣latency␣
    from␣the␣client.␣This␣preference␣is␣useful␣for␣reducing␣overall␣latency␣
    and␣distributing␣the␣read␣load␣equally␣among␣nodes,␣but␣it␣may␣lead␣to␣
    the␣read␣of␣outdated␣data,␣and␣possibly␣stale␣or␣inconsistent␣results,␣
    and␣may␣not␣be␣appropriate␣for␣writes.
```

The choice of read preference will depend on the requirements of the application, the use case or the querying patterns. For operations requiring immediate data consistency for updates or inserts, the 'primary' or 'primaryPreferred' read preferences will provide the most accurate data. Meanwhile, when data consistency is not the primary concern, like analytics queries, 'secondary' or 'secondaryPreferred' can be utilized, distributing the read workload across the secondary nodes, while keeping the primary focused on writes.

```
// Example
// create a Mongo client
const MongoClient = require('mongodb').MongoClient;
const uri = 'mongodb://localhost:27017/test?replicaSet=rs0';
const client = new MongoClient(uri);

// create a collection instance
const collection = client.db('test').collection('inventory');
// insert some test documents
await collection.insertMany([
  {item: 'pen', qty: 100},
  {item: 'notebook', qty: 200},
  {item: 'pencil', qty: 50}
]);

// connect with primary read preference
const primaryReadPref = new MongoClient(client, {
  readPreference: 'primary'
});
await primaryReadPref.connect();

// try to read from a secondary with a read preference
const secondaryReadPref = new MongoClient(client, {
  readPreference: 'secondaryPreferred'
});
await secondaryReadPref.connect();
```

5.14   How do you configure and use MongoDB Ops Manager for managing and monitoring MongoDB deployments?

MongoDB Ops Manager is a tool that provides a centralized management, monitoring, and backup solution for MongoDB deployments. It is an on-premise tool that can be set up in a few scenarios, including as a standalone instance, or as a cluster.

Here are the steps to set up and configure MongoDB Ops Manager:

1. **Download and Install:** Download the MongoDB Ops Manager package from the official website, and install it on a dedicated server or a cluster of servers. MongoDB provides installation guides for different platforms like Linux, macOS, and Windows.

2. **Configure MongoDB Deployment:** To manage a MongoDB deployment using MongoDB Ops Manager, we need to configure the MongoDB deployment in the Ops Manager. The configuration includes adding the MongoDB deployment as a resource with details like hostname, port, and authentication credentials.

3. **Add Monitoring Agents:** The MongoDB Ops Manager uses Monitoring Agents to monitor the MongoDB deployment. We need to install Monitoring Agents on every MongoDB server. For this, we have to download the appropriate package from the Ops Manager, and then install and configure it on each MongoDB server.

4. **Create Alert Configurations:** Mongo Ops Manager sends alerts when a specific event or condition occurs, such as when a server goes down, connections become unavailable, or replication lag increases. We can create custom alert configurations to monitor events that are relevant to us.

5. **Create Backup Configurations:** In addition to monitoring, MongoDB Ops Manager provides automated backup management. We can create backup configurations that automatically backup the MongoDB deployment at scheduled intervals.

6. **View and Analyze:** We can use the MongoDB Ops Manager interface to view and analyze the metrics and statistics collected by the monitoring agents. We can also use the interface to view backups, restore backups, and perform other management tasks.

Here is an example of how to add a MongoDB deployment as a resource to MongoDB Ops Manager:

1. Navigate to the Ops Manager dashboard, and click the "Add" button in the "Deployment" section.

2. Choose "MongoDB" as the deployment type, and enter the host-name, port, and authentication information for the MongoDB deployment.

3. Click the "Test" button to test the connection, and then click "Save."

4. On the following screen, we can specify the location of the monitoring agent, and download it to the respective server.

5. Restart the MongoDB server to complete the process.

Here is an example of how to use MongoDB Ops Manager to create a backup configuration:

1. Navigate to the Ops Manager dashboard, and click the "Add" button in the "Backups" section.

2. Choose the MongoDB deployment that we want to back up, and then click "Next."

3. Specify the backup configuration options, such as backup frequency, retention period, backup method, and storage location.

4. Click "Save" to save the backup configuration.

In conclusion, MongoDB Ops Manager provides a simple and effective solution for managing and monitoring MongoDB deployments. Its features like monitoring, automation of backups, alerting and security management simplify the process of managing MongoDB deployments.

5.15   Describe the process of tuning MongoDB server settings for optimal performance and resource usage.

Tuning MongoDB server settings is an important process that can significantly improve the performance of applications that use MongoDB. In this answer, we will discuss the process of tuning MongoDB server settings for optimal performance and resource usage.

1. Identify the bottleneck:
The first step in tuning MongoDB is to identify the bottleneck. A
bottleneck can be a slow query, high CPU usage, high disk I/O, etc.
MongoDB provides various tools to monitor the performance of the
database, such as mongostat, mongotop, and the MongoDB profiler.
These tools can help identify the bottleneck(s) and allow you to focus
your efforts on the areas that need improvement.

2. Identify the hardware:
The second step is to identify the hardware on which the MongoDB
server is running. The performance of MongoDB is closely tied to the
hardware on which it is running. The hardware factors that are most
important for MongoDB are RAM, CPU, and disk I/O. The more
memory and cores that are available, the faster the database will run.
It is also important to ensure that the disk is fast enough to handle
the I/O load of the database.

3. Adjust the cache size:
The cache size is one of the most important settings in MongoDB.
MongoDB uses memory-mapped files to manage the data in the database.
The cache size determines how much of that data can be kept in memory. By default, MongoDB will use half of the available memory for
the cache. However, this may not be optimal for all workloads. For
example, if the database is mostly read-heavy, it may be beneficial to
increase the cache size to improve read performance. On the other
hand, if the database is write-heavy, it may be beneficial to reduce
the cache size to improve write performance.

4. Adjust the write concern:
The write concern determines how MongoDB handles write operations. MongoDB allows you to specify different write concerns depending on your application requirements. By default, write operations will wait for acknowledgment from one server. However, you
can increase the write concern to wait for acknowledgment from multiple servers or even wait for the write to be replicated to a certain
number of servers before continuing. This can significantly impact
the performance of the database.

5. Adjust the read preference:
The read preference determines how MongoDB handles read operations. MongoDB allows you to specify different read preferences
depending on your application requirements. By default, read opera-

tions will distribute evenly across all available servers. However, you can specify that read operations should prefer certain servers based on their proximity or their data center. This can help optimize read performance if your application has specific requirements.

6. Adjust the index configuration:
Indexes are critical for good performance in MongoDB. MongoDB provides various types of indexes, such as single-field indexes, compound indexes, and geospatial indexes. By default, MongoDB will automatically create an index on the _id field. However, you may need to create additional indexes to support your application's queries. Creating too many indexes can impact write performance, while creating too few indexes can impact read performance.

7. Monitor and adjust:
Once you have made changes to the MongoDB server settings, it is important to monitor the performance of the database to ensure that the changes have had the desired impact. MongoDB provides various tools to monitor the performance of the database, such as mongostat, mongotop, and the MongoDB profiler. If the changes have not had the desired impact, you may need to adjust the settings further.

In conclusion, tuning MongoDB server settings requires careful consideration of various factors such as hardware, cache size, write concern, read preference, index configuration, etc. It is important to monitor the performance of the database continually and make adjustments as necessary to ensure optimal performance and resource usage.

5.16 How do you handle hotspots in a MongoDB sharded cluster, and what are the strategies to minimize their impact on performance?

In a MongoDB sharded cluster, hotspots can occur when a large number of read or write operations are concentrated on a single shard or a few shards rather than being distributed across the entire cluster. Hotspots can lead to poor performance and can cause the affected shard(s) to become overwhelmed, potentially resulting in downtime.

To handle hotspots in a MongoDB sharded cluster, there are several strategies that can be employed:

1. Rebalancing the Shard Key Range:
MongoDB uses a shard key to distribute data across the shards in a cluster. If the distribution of data is not even, some shards can become hotspots. To address this issue, the shard key range can be rebalanced to evenly distribute data across the cluster. This can be done by choosing an appropriate shard key and adjusting the range values for the shard key.

2. Adding Indexes:
Adding indexes to collections can help to optimize query performance and distribute the workload across the shards in a cluster. Indexes can help to avoid table scans and improve query performance, which can help to reduce the workload on hot shards.

3. Adding Shards:
Adding additional shards to the cluster can help to distribute the workload and reduce hotspots. When adding new shards, it is important to consider the distribution of data across the shards and to place the new shards in a way that balances the workload.

4. Caching:
Caching can help to reduce the workload on hot shards by storing frequently accessed data in memory. This can help to reduce the number of queries that need to be executed, which can reduce the load on the hot shard(s).

5. Query Optimization:
Optimizing queries can help to reduce the amount of data that needs to be processed and distributed across the shards in a cluster. Optimizing queries can help to reduce the workload on hot shards and improve overall query performance.

To minimize the impact of hotspots on performance in a MongoDB sharded cluster, it is important to identify hotspots early and take corrective action as soon as possible. Monitoring the workload on each shard and using tools such as the MongoDB profiler to identify performance bottlenecks can help to prevent hotspots from occurring. Additionally, regular capacity planning and load testing can help to identify potential hotspots and ensure that the cluster is configured appropriately to handle increases in workload.

5.17 Explain the process of setting up and managing MongoDB encryption at rest and in transit for data security.

MongoDB provides built-in support for encryption of data at rest and in transit, ensuring confidentiality and integrity of data stored in a MongoDB deployment.

To set up encryption at rest, MongoDB provides multiple options for encrypting the storage engine, including encryption at the file-level, encryption using OS-level encryption, and encryption using device-level encryption. MongoDB Enterprise Edition also provides field-level encryption, which allows specific fields within a document to be encrypted independently.

Here's an overview of the steps involved in setting up encryption at rest in a MongoDB deployment:

1. Choose the appropriate encryption option based on your environment and security needs.

2. Generate encryption keys and certificates as needed.

3. Set up MongoDB with the encryption settings, including configuring the storage engine to use encryption and setting up field-level encryption.

4. Ensure all clients that access the MongoDB deployment have the necessary certificates and keys to connect to the encrypted deployment.

To set up encryption in transit, MongoDB provides SSL/TLS encryption options that can be configured for client-server connections, inter-node connections in a replica set, and inter-cluster connections in a sharded cluster.

Here's an overview of the steps involved in setting up encryption in transit in a MongoDB deployment:

1. Obtain or create SSL/TLS certificates for each node in the MongoDB deployment.

2. Enable SSL/TLS settings in the MongoDB configuration file or via command line options.

3. Configure clients to use SSL/TLS encryption when connecting to the MongoDB deployment.

Here's an example of enabling SSL/TLS encryption in a MongoDB deployment:

```
# Enable SSL/TLS encryption via configuration file
net:
  ssl:
    mode: requireSSL
    PEMKeyFile: /path/to/server.pem
    CAFile: /path/to/ca.pem

# Enable SSL/TLS encryption via command line option
mongod --sslMode requireSSL --sslPEMKeyFile /path/to/server.pem --sslCAFile /
    path/to/ca.pem
```

MongoDB also provides auditing capabilities to track database activity and monitor security-related events. The audit log can be configured to capture events related to access control, authentication, and authorization, providing an additional layer of security for MongoDB deployments.

In summary, MongoDB provides robust built-in capabilities for encrypting data at rest and in transit and auditing database activity for increased data security. It's important to carefully consider the appropriate encryption options based on your environment and security needs and to properly configure clients to use encryption when connecting to the MongoDB deployment.

5.18   How can you use MongoDB's full-text search capabilities to perform complex text-based queries?

MongoDB has several features to perform full-text searches using text indexes which can greatly enhance the performance and accuracy of text-based queries on large documents that require more than just an exact match. In order to use these features effectively, it is essential

to create a text index on the collection and select the appropriate text
search operators that best fit the search requirements. In addition,
it is important to understand how MongoDB ranks the relevance of
text search results.

Here are some steps to perform complex text-based queries using
MongoDB's full-text search capabilities:

1. Create a Text Index on the Collection:

To enable full-text search on a collection, a text index must be created
on one or more fields that contains text data. This can be done using
the 'createIndex()' method with the 'text' option set to 'true'. Below
is an example:

```
db.collection.createIndex({ field: "text" })
```

In this example, the 'createIndex()' method creates a text index on
the 'field' attribute of the collection.

2. Search for Exact Phrases:

One of the simplest types of text search queries is to find a specific
word or phrase within a collection. To search for an exact phrase,
the '$text' operator can be used in conjunction with the '$search'
operator. For example:

```
db.collection.find({ $text: { $search: "word1␣word2" } })
```

This query will search for documents containing the exact phrase
"word1 word2".

3. Search for Any of the Words:

To search for documents containing any of the specified words, the
'$in' operator can be used along with the '$text' and '$search' oper-
ators. For example:

```
db.collection.find({ $text: { $search: "word1␣word2" }, field: { $in: ["word1
", "word2"] } })
```

This query will search for documents containing either "word1" or
"word2" within the 'field'.

4. Search for All of the Words:

To search for documents containing all of the specified words, the '$all'
operator can be used along with the '$text' and '$search' operators.
For example:

```
db.collection.find({ $text: { $search: ""word1"␣"word2"" } })
```

This query will search for documents containing both "word1" and
"word2". Note the use of quotes around the search terms to indicate
that the terms should be searched as a phrase.

5. Use Stop Words:

Stop words are common words (such as "the", "and", "but", etc.) that
are ignored by the text search engine. By default, MongoDB supports
several languages and automatically removes stop words. However,
if it is necessary to search for stop words in a specific language, they
can be included in the search query by using the '$language' operator.
For example:

```
db.collection.find({ $text: { $search: "the␣and␣but", $language: "english" }
    })
```

This query will search for documents containing the stop words "the",
"and", and "but" in English.

6. Rank Search Results:

MongoDB assigns a relevance score to each search result based on how
closely the search terms match the indexed text. The relevance score
is calculated using a combination of factors, including the frequency
of the search terms in the text, the length of the text, and the location
of the search terms within the text. The '$meta' operator can be used
to retrieve and sort results by the relevance score. For example:

```
db.collection.find({ $text: { $search: "word1␣word2" } }, { score: { $meta: "
    textScore" } }).sort({ score: { $meta: "textScore" } })
```

This query will retrieve documents containing the search terms "word1"
and "word2" and sort them by relevance score.

In summary, MongoDB's full-text search capabilities can greatly enhance the performance and accuracy of text-based queries on large

collections. By creating a text index, selecting appropriate search operators, and understanding how MongoDB ranks the relevance of search results, complex text-based queries can be executed efficiently and accurately.

5.19 Describe the role of a MongoDB arbiter in a replica set, and discuss the implications of using an arbiter in production environments.

In a MongoDB replica set, the primary node is responsible for handling all write operations and forwarding read operations to the other nodes. The secondary nodes replicate the data from the primary and can be used to handle read operations as well. However, in some cases, it may not be feasible or necessary to have an even number of nodes in the replica set. In such cases, an arbiter can be added to the replica set.

An arbiter node in a MongoDB replica set is a special type of node that does not store any data. Its primary function is to participate in the voting process that determines which node will become the primary in case the current primary node becomes unavailable. When a primary node fails, the remaining nodes in the replica set form an election to determine the new primary. Each node casts a vote for the node it thinks should become the new primary, and the node with the majority vote is elected as the new primary. An arbiter is used to ensure there is always an odd number of votes, so a majority can always be reached.

Adding an arbiter to a replica set has several implications for production environments. First, it can help to prevent split-brain scenarios, where two nodes think they are the primary and start accepting write operations. In such scenarios, data can become inconsistent and difficult to reconcile. By ensuring there is always an odd number of votes, an arbiter can help prevent split-brain scenarios from occurring.

Second, using an arbiter can reduce the cost and complexity of the replica set. Without an arbiter, a replica set would need to have an even number of nodes to prevent split-brain scenarios. This would mean increasing the number of secondary nodes, which can be expensive in terms of hardware and maintenance costs. Adding an arbiter helps reduce the number of nodes required, which can lower costs and simplify the configuration.

However, there are also some potential drawbacks to using an arbiter. For one, an arbiter does not provide any data redundancy, since it does not store any data. This means that if one of the other nodes fail, there will be no secondary node to take over as primary. Additionally, adding an arbiter can introduce additional network traffic and latency, since it will need to participate in the voting process.

In summary, an arbiter node in a MongoDB replica set is a special node that participates in the voting process used to elect a new primary in case of a failure. Using an arbiter can help prevent split-brain scenarios and simplify the configuration of the replica set. However, it does not provide any data redundancy and can introduce additional network traffic and latency. Whether to use an arbiter or not depends on the specific needs of the application and the trade-offs between cost, complexity, and redundancy.

5.20   What are the best practices for ensuring high availability and failover in a MongoDB sharded cluster?

To ensure high availability and failover in a MongoDB sharded cluster, there are several best practices that you can follow:

1. Set up replica sets: In a sharded environment, each shard should have a minimum of three (3) nodes configured as a replica set for fault tolerance. This helps to ensure that data is continuously available in the event of a primary replica set node failure. You can set up replica sets by using the rs.initiate() method.

2. Use a configuration replica set: A dedicated replica set should be used to store the cluster's metadata, such as the configuration data and shard key ranges. This replica set should have a minimum of three (3) nodes to ensure high availability. You can set up a configuration

replica set by using the sh.addShard() method.

3. Monitor the health of the cluster: To prevent failures, you need to continually monitor the health of the cluster. MongoDB offers monitoring tools like Ops Manager and Cloud Manager. You can also use serverStatus and replSetGetStatus methods to get cluster health information programmatically. If any node or replica set goes down, you will get an alert and take necessary actions to recover the failed node.

4. Use shard key optimization: Proper shard key selection is critical to the performance and scalability of the sharded cluster. The chosen shard key should be uniformly distributed across all shards to prevent hotspots. MongoDB 4.4 introduces intelligent global clustering to help auto-select the right shard key based on popular queries and traffic.

5. Use graceful shutdowns: If you need to take a node or a shard offline, use a graceful shutdown. This ensures that the node is removed from the cluster without causing data loss or significant performance degradation. You can use the sh.removeShard() method to remove a shard.

6. Test failovers and recoveries: It's essential to test failovers and recoveries regularly to ensure that the system can withstand failures. You should run simulated failovers and recoveries during off-peak times to evaluate the effectiveness of the failover procedures.

Overall, following these best practices will ensure that your MongoDB sharded cluster is highly available and fault-tolerant.

Chapter 6

Guru

6.1 xplain the Write-Ahead Logging (WAL) mechanism in MongoDB's WiredTiger storage engine and its implications for performance and data durability.

The WiredTiger storage engine in MongoDB uses the Write-Ahead Logging (WAL) mechanism to ensure data durability and improve write performance. In this mechanism, instead of directly writing data to disk, changes are first written to a log file on disk called the WAL. Once the changes are recorded in the WAL, they are applied to the database files in the background.

The WAL serves several purposes in WiredTiger. First, it ensures that write operations are durable, meaning that they are persisted to disk and can survive server failures or crashes. When MongoDB performs a write operation, it writes the changes to the WAL first. If the write operation is successful, it is guaranteed to be durable since it is in the log file. If the server crashes before the write operation is applied to the database files, MongoDB can recover the data by replaying the changes from the log file.

Second, the use of the WAL improves write performance in WiredTiger.

By separating the write operations into two phases, the application
can continue to write data to the WAL while the data is being applied
to the database files. This allows the application to perform multiple
write operations concurrently, improving throughput and reducing
latency.

However, using the WAL does have some implications for MongoDB's
performance. Writing data to the WAL and applying the changes to
the database files requires additional I/O operations, which can increase latency and reduce the overall performance of write operations.
In addition, the size of the WAL can also impact performance. If the
WAL size is too small, MongoDB may need to flush the logs to disk
more frequently, which can impact write performance. On the other
hand, if the WAL size is too large, it can consume significant disk
space and potentially impact the performance of read operations.

To optimize performance and data durability with the WAL in WiredTiger,
it is recommended to tune the WAL size and other configuration parameters based on the workload and available resources. For example, increasing the WAL size can improve write performance if there
is enough disk space available, while decreasing the size can reduce
latency and improve performance if the workload is write-heavy. Additionally, enabling compression for the log file can reduce disk usage
and improve performance. Overall, the use of the WAL in MongoDB
provides a reliable and high-performance mechanism for securing data
and ensuring durability in the face of failures.

6.2   Discuss the potential trade-offs of us-ing different compression algorithms (Snappy, zlib, or zstd) in MongoDB's WiredTiger storage engine.

MongoDB's WiredTiger storage engine provides support for three different compression algorithms - Snappy, zlib, and zstd. Each of these
compression algorithms has its own set of advantages and disadvantages which must be considered carefully in order to select the most
appropriate algorithm for a given use case.

Snappy is a fast and lightweight compression algorithm which is well-suited for use cases in which data needs to be compressed and decompressed quickly with minimal CPU overhead. Snappy is particularly well-suited for use with data which is already highly compressed or in situations in which the compression ratio is not particularly important.

One potential trade-off of using Snappy is that it may not offer the highest possible compression ratios compared to other compression algorithms. This means that if storage space is at a premium and compression ratios are a critical factor, another compression algorithm may be a better choice.

Zlib is a widely-used compression algorithm which provides a good balance between compression ratio and CPU usage. Zlib can achieve higher compression ratios than Snappy while still providing relatively fast compression and decompression times.

One potential trade-off of using zlib is that it may consume more CPU resources than Snappy. This means that in situations in which CPU resources are limited and compressing and decompressing data quickly is not a critical factor, using Snappy or another lightweight compression algorithm may be a better choice.

Zstd is a relatively new compression algorithm which provides potentially higher compression ratios than zlib while still providing fast compression and decompression times. Zstd is particularly well-suited for use cases in which the compression ratio is a critical factor.

One potential trade-off of using Zstd is that it may consume more CPU resources than both Snappy and zlib. This means that in situations in which CPU resources are limited, using Zstd may not be a good choice.

In conclusion, the trade-offs of using Snappy, zlib, or Zstd in the WiredTiger storage engine depend on a variety of factors, including the specific use case, the importance of compression ratio and speed, and the available CPU resources. Therefore, selecting the most appropriate compression algorithm requires careful consideration of these factors. Below is an example of how to configure compression options in MongoDB's WiredTiger storage engine:

```
mongo --eval 'db.adminCommand(␣{␣setParameter:␣1,␣compression:␣{␣compressors:
```

```
␣["zlib",␣"zstd"],␣blockCompressor:␣"zlib",␣zlibCompressionLevel:␣6,␣
zlibStrategy:␣0␣}␣}␣}␣)'
```

6.3   How does MongoDB's causal consistency guarantee work, and what are its implications for read and write operations?

Causal consistency is a consistency model used in distributed systems where causal relationships between operations must be preserved. In MongoDB, it ensures that a write operation always propagates to all nodes in the system before any subsequent read operation can retrieve the modified data.

In more detail, when an application writes to MongoDB, it specifies a 'write concern' that determines how many nodes must acknowledge the write before it is considered committed. If a write concern has a 'majority' setting, it means that the write must be acknowledged by a majority of the nodes in the cluster, which guarantees that the write has propagated to all nodes in the system. Once the write is successful, the client will receive a special acknowledgement known as a 'write concern acknowledgement'.

When a client executes a read operation, it specifies a 'read concern' that determines which visibility guarantees MongoDB will provide. A 'majority' read concern ensures that a read operation will always see the most recently committed data from a majority of the nodes in the system, which ensures that all prior writes are visible. These guarantees are provided by a logical clock system that tracks the order of operations and their dependencies.

The implications of causal consistency for read and write operations are that:

1. Write operations can be slower because they must propagate to a majority of the nodes before they are considered committed. However, this ensures that subsequent read operations will always see the most recently committed data.

2. Read operations can be optimized if the client knows that the data being read was previously written by the same client. In this case, the client can specify a 'snapshot read concern' that will guarantee that the read operation only sees the writes made by that client. This avoids the need to propagate the write to a majority of nodes, which can be faster.

3. In multi-document transactions, MongoDB will ensure that all operations in the transaction are causally consistent, which means that they will be executed in a way that preserves their causal relationships.

Overall, causal consistency is a useful consistency model for distributed systems that require strong guarantees about the causality of operations. However, it comes at the cost of slower write operations, which may not be a good match for systems that require high write throughput.

6.4 Describe the process of implementing a custom collation for sorting and searching text data in MongoDB.

MongoDB supports custom collations that allow you to define your own rules for sorting and searching text data. This enables you to take into account language-specific or domain-specific conventions for sorting and searching text data.

The process of implementing a custom collation in MongoDB has several steps:

1. Define the custom collation rules: You need to define the rules for sorting and searching text data according to your requirements. This involves defining the order in which characters should be sorted and the way in which characters with diacritical marks or other accents should be handled.

2. Create a collation object in MongoDB: You need to create a collation object in MongoDB that describes your custom collation rules. This is done using the collation option in the relevant MongoDB query

or operation. The collation object can include a variety of options such as strength, case sensitivity, and numeric order.

Here is an example of a collation object that sets the collation to French and case-insensitive:

```
{ collation: { locale: "fr", strength: 1, caseLevel: false } }
```

3. Use the collation option in queries: Once you have defined your custom collation rules and created a collation object in MongoDB, you can use the collation option in your MongoDB queries to apply your custom collation. For example, the following query applies the custom collation to a find operation:

```
db.collection.find({ name: "John" }).collation({ collation: { locale: "fr",
    strength: 1, caseLevel: false } })
```

This query applies the French collation to the name field and retrieves all documents that have "John" as the name, using the custom collation rules for sorting and searching.

4. Create an index with collation: You may also want to create an index with your custom collation rules to improve query performance. This can be done by adding the collation option to the createIndex operation. For example:

```
db.collection.createIndex({ name: 1 }, { collation: { locale: "fr", strength:
    1, caseLevel: false } })
```

This creates an index on the name field with the French collation and the custom collation rules for sorting and searching.

In summary, implementing a custom collation in MongoDB involves defining your collation rules, creating a collation object in MongoDB, using the collation option in queries, and optionally creating an index with collation.

6.5   Explain the impact of various MongoDB server settings on connection management and resource usage, such as maxIncomingConnections, maxPoolSize, and waitQueueTimeoutMS.

MongoDB server settings greatly affect how a MongoDB deployment uses server resources, such as connections and pools. Here are some of the MongoDB server settings that can affect connection management and resource usage:

1. maxIncomingConnections: This setting determines the maximum number of incoming connections that MongoDB can handle simultaneously. If this limit is set too low, clients will be unable to connect to the database, which could cause problems with the application using the database. If this limit is set too high, the MongoDB server could run out of system resources, such as file descriptors or memory. The default value for maxIncomingConnections is 511, which should be sufficient for most applications.

2. maxPoolSize: This setting determines the maximum number of connections that a connection pool can open simultaneously. The connection pool is a collection of reusable connections that are available to service the application's requests. If the application tries to open more connections than allowed by this setting, MongoDB will reject the connection request. This setting is useful for controlling the use of system resources such as file descriptors, memory, and CPU. Setting the maximum pool size too high can cause the application to use more resources than necessary, while setting it too low can cause the application to miss opportunities to use free resources. The recommended value for maxPoolSize is proportional to the number of threads or connections your application creates.

3. waitQueueTimeoutMS: This setting defines the maximum time a new request can wait in the wait queue before timing out. When the connection pool is full, MongoDB will hold incoming client requests in a queue until a connection becomes available. If the requests wait too long, the client may disconnect, causing additional load on the database. The default value of waitQueueTimeoutMS is

120,000 milliseconds or two minutes. Setting this value to a shorter
period may improve application responsiveness, but at the cost of an
increased number of connection attempts. This value should be adjusted according to the latency of the client requests and the number
of connections in the pool.

Here is an example of using these settings in MongoDB's native driver
for Node.js:

```
const MongoClient = require('mongodb').MongoClient;

const url = 'mongodb://localhost:27017';
const dbName = 'myproject';

const client = new MongoClient(url, {
  useNewUrlParser: true,
  useUnifiedTopology: true,
  poolSize: 10, // set the size of the connection pool
  maxPoolSize: 50, // set the maximum number of connections in the pool
  keepAlive: true, // keep idle connections alive to improve latency
  socketTimeoutMS: 30000, // set the maximum time for sockets to timeout
  connectTimeoutMS: 10000, // set the maximum time for a connection attempt to
        timeout
  waitQueueTimeoutMS: 2000, // set the maximum time for new requests to wait
        in the queue
  autoReconnect: true, // automatically try to reconnect if the connection is
        lost
  appname: 'myapp', // set the application name to identify connections in the
        server logs
});

client.connect((err) => {
  if (err) {
    console.log(err);
    process.exit(1);
  }
  console.log('Connected successfully to server');
  const db = client.db(dbName);

  // do something with the database

  client.close();
});
```

In this example, the poolSize is set to 10, which means that the connection pool starts with 10 connections. The maxPoolSize is set to 50,
which means that the connection pool can open up to 50 connections.
The waitQueueTimeoutMS is set to 2000, which means that a new
request can wait in the queue for up to two seconds before timing out.
These settings can be adjusted according to the requirements of the
application, the resources available on the server, and the expected
usage patterns of the application.

6.6 Discuss the challenges and best practices for implementing a MongoDB change data capture (CDC) mechanism to propagate data changes to other systems.

One of the common use cases for MongoDB is to use it as a source of data that needs to be propagated to other systems. This can be achieved using change data capture (CDC) mechanisms. The CDC mechanism tracks data changes in the MongoDB database and propagates them to other systems. In this way, the changes in the MongoDB database are automatically reflected in the other systems. In this answer, we will discuss the challenges involved in implementing MongoDB CDC and best practices to overcome them.

Challenges involved in implementing MongoDB CDC:
1. Data Consistency: MongoDB CDC mechanism should ensure data consistency between the source database and the target systems. As the changes are propagated asynchronously, it's important to ensure that data is not lost or corrupted during propagation.

2. High Performance: The CDC mechanism should not impact the performance of the MongoDB database. If the CDC process is slow, it may cause delays in propagating changes to the target systems, leading to inconsistent data.

3. Data Transformation: The data format stored in MongoDB may not be compatible with the target systems. The CDC mechanism needs to transform the data into the required format for the target systems.

4. Error Handling: The CDC mechanism should have robust error handling to handle any errors during propagation, including network failures or data transformation errors.

5. Scalability: As the size of the MongoDB database grows, the CDC mechanism should scale accordingly. It should be able to handle the increasing volume of changes in a timely manner.

Best Practices for implementing MongoDB CDC:
1. Schema Design: To ensure data consistency, it's essential to follow

a consistent schema design. The schema design should be optimized for the CDC mechanism, with appropriate indexes, shard keys, and document structures. This will help reduce the time required to capture and transform the data for propagation.

2. Use Change Streams: MongoDB provides a built-in feature called Change Streams that can be used to track changes in a database. Change Streams can be used to capture changes in near-real-time, reducing the latency in propagating changes to the target systems.

3. Use Appropriate CDC Tool: There are various CDC tools available in the market that can be used to propagate data changes from MongoDB to other systems. Before selecting a CDC tool, evaluate it based on your specific use case and requirements. Some popular CDC tools for MongoDB include Debezium, Apache Kafka, and MongoDB Connector for Apache Kafka.

4. Transform Data: Data transformation is an essential step in the CDC process. The CDC mechanism needs to transform the data in MongoDB into the required format for the target systems. MongoDB provides various data transformation tools such as MongoDB Connector for BI, and MongoDB Connector for Spark.

5. Error Handling: To handle error scenarios during CDC, it is important to have a robust error handling mechanism. When an error occurs, it's important to log the error, retry the operation, and send notifications to the relevant stakeholders.

6. Monitor Performance: Monitoring performance of the CDC mechanism is important to ensure that it doesn't impact the performance of the MongoDB database. Monitoring can help identify bottlenecks and scaling issues, enabling pro-active action to optimize performance.

In conclusion, implementing MongoDB CDC requires careful consideration of all the challenges mentioned above. By following the best practices discussed, you can ensure that your CDC mechanism is robust, scalable, and provides near real-time data propagation from MongoDB to other systems.

6.7 How do you use the $reduce operator in the MongoDB aggregation framework to perform complex data transformation tasks?

The '$reduce' operator in the MongoDB aggregation framework provides a way to apply a custom operation on an array field and returns the final result of the operation. It is useful in situations where we need to traverse an array field, perform some calculations on each element, and return either a single value or a modified array.

The syntax for '$reduce' is as follows:

```
{ $reduce: {
    input: <array>,
    initialValue: <initialValue>,
    in: <operation>
}}
```

where:

- 'input': specifies the array field on which we want to apply the operation.

- 'initialValue': specifies the initial value to be used in the operation.

- 'in': specifies the operation to be performed on each element of the array. It can be any valid aggregation expression.

Here is an example of using '$reduce':

Suppose we have a collection of documents representing sales of different products:

```
{
  "_id": 1,
  "product": "A",
  "sales": [10, 20, 30]
},
{
  "_id": 2,
  "product": "B",
  "sales": [5, 15, 25, 35]
},
{
  "_id": 3,
  "product": "C",
  "sales": [40, 50]
}
```

Let's say we want to calculate the total number of sales for each product. We can use '$reduce' to sum up the elements of the 'sales' array for each document using the following pipeline:

```
db.sales.aggregate([
  {
    $project: {
      _id: 0,
      product: 1,
      totalSales: {
        $reduce: {
          input: "$sales",
          initialValue: 0,
          in: { $add: ["$$value", "$$this"] }
        }
      }
    }
  }
])
```

The '$project' stage includes two fields in the output: 'product' and 'totalSales'. The '$reduce' operator is used to sum up the elements of the 'sales' array for each document. The '$$value' variable represents the running total, which is initialized with '0' ('$$initialValue'). The '$$this' variable represents the current element of the array being processed.

The output of the above aggregation pipeline will be:

```
{ "product" : "A", "totalSales" : 60 }
{ "product" : "B", "totalSales" : 80 }
{ "product" : "C", "totalSales" : 90 }
```

As we can see, '$reduce' is a powerful operator that allows us to perform complex data transformations on array fields. By combining it with other operators and stages in the aggregation framework, we can achieve a wide range of data analyses and manipulations.

6.8 Describe strategies for modeling and querying time-series data in MongoDB to optimize storage and query performance.

Time-series data is a type of data where measurements are taken continuously over time. In a typical scenario, time-series data is generated by sensors or devices, and the data is collected and stored for further analysis. MongoDB is a database management system that can be used to store and manage time-series data, providing features for efficient storage and querying of this type of data. Here are some strategies for modeling and querying time-series data in MongoDB to optimize storage and query performance.

1. Model the data using a time-series schema

MongoDB supports various data modeling strategies, but to optimize storage and query performance for time-series data, it is recommended to use a time-series schema. This involves organizing the data into buckets based on time intervals, for example, 1 minute, 5 minutes, or 15 minutes. The data for each time interval can be stored in a document, with fields for the timestamp, measurements, and other metadata. Using a time-series schema can reduce the number of documents that need to be accessed and the amount of data that needs to be scanned during queries, improving query performance.

Here is an example of a time-series schema in MongoDB:

```
{
  "timestamp": ISODate("2021-05-01T12:00:00.000Z"),
  "interval": "5 minutes",
  "measurements": {
    "temperature": [25.0, 24.5, 24.3, 24.8, 25.2],
    "humidity": [60, 55, 50, 48, 45]
  },
  "metadata": {
    "sensor_id": "12345",
    "location": "office"
  }
}
```

2. Use indexes to improve query performance

To improve query performance, it is important to create indexes on the fields that are frequently used in queries. For time-series data, this could include the timestamp and other metadata fields. Indexes can help to reduce the number of documents that need to be scanned during queries, improving query performance.

Here is an example of creating an index on the timestamp field:

```
db.measurements.createIndex({ timestamp: 1 })
```

3. Use aggregation pipelines to process time-series data

Aggregation pipelines are a powerful feature of MongoDB that can be used to process and analyze time-series data. Aggregation pipelines allow you to combine multiple stages of data processing into a single query, improving query performance and reducing the amount of data that needs to be transferred between the server and client. Aggregation pipelines can be used to group data by time intervals, calculate averages, sums, and other aggregates, and perform other calculations and transformations on time-series data.

Here is an example of an aggregation pipeline that groups data by day and calculates the average temperature for each day:

```
db.measurements.aggregate([
  { $group: {
    _id: { $dateToString: { format: "%Y-%m-%d", date: "$timestamp" } },
    avg_temperature: { $avg: "$measurements.temperature" }
  }}
])
```

In this example, the data is first grouped by the date portion of the timestamp field using the $dateToString$ operator. Then, the avg operator is used to calculate the average temperature for each group.

In summary, to optimize storage and query performance for time-series data in MongoDB, it is recommended to use a time-series schema, create indexes on frequently-used fields, and use aggregation pipelines to process and analyze the data. These strategies can help to reduce the amount of data that needs to be scanned during queries, improve query performance, and enable efficient storage and retrieval of time-series data in MongoDB.

6.9 Discuss the potential challenges and best practices for deploying and managing a global MongoDB cluster with multiple data centers and regions.

Deploying and managing a global MongoDB cluster with multiple data centers and regions can bring a lot of benefits to an organization, such as lower response latency, improved fault tolerance, and compliance with data sovereignty requirements. However, this can also introduce several challenges that need to be addressed to ensure the cluster's optimal performance and availability. In this answer, we will discuss some of these challenges and best practices.

Challenges:

1. **Network Latency**: When working with a distributed cluster, network latency between different data centers can play a significant role in overall performance. MongoDB relies heavily on network communication for replication, sharding, and failover, so high latency can impact the responsiveness and accuracy of the system, increasing the chances of inconsistencies and conflicts.

2. **Data Consistency**: With a distributed cluster, data consistency can become an issue because different data centers may receive different updates at different times. This can result in conflicts and data inconsistencies, especially during updates or deletes.

3. **Fault Tolerance**: Having multiple data centers can increase the fault tolerance of the system. However, it also raises several other questions such as how to ensure that data is always available, how to handle network partitioning problems, and how to ensure automatic failovers.

4. **Data Privacy and Security**: With data being distributed across multiple regions, data privacy and security measures can become more complicated. Organizations relying on MongoDB will need to consider how to protect data from local legal and regulatory environments, whether to enforce centralized authentication or let individual data centers manage their own security settings.

Best practices:

1. **Limit Geographic Distribution**: One of the best practices for dealing with network latency and data consistency is to limit the geographic distribution of the cluster. Allowing too many data centers and regions to participate in the same database operations can result in unreliable and slow performance. A good rule of thumb is to ensure that data centers participating in the same MongoDB cluster are within the same continent or region.

2. **Use appropriate Sharding**: Sharding can help with the performance and scalability of the cluster but can also introduce new challenges in the form of network latency and data consistency. An appropriate sharding key chosen from within the data model can constrain the data to a specific shard and reduce the need for cross-regional communication.

3. **Ensure Logical vs. Physical Data Separation**: Separating data according to logical dimensions and not necessarily physical ones can help with data consistency and data privacy. This practice may involve subdividing data into different collections or databases that conform to a logical partitioning key.

4. **Use Secondary Regions for Disaster Recovery**: MongoDB supports secondary regions, which can be used for disaster recovery while the primary region is down. Replica sets can be configured to replicate data to secondary regions, supporting failover if the primary goes offline or is unavailable. Hence, it's imperative to have secondary regions located in different geographical locations from the primary region.

5. **Configure Read Preferences**: Read preferences are configurations that control from where to read data from replica sets. These are particularly useful for geographical partitioning, allowing you to read data from a data center nearer to the user. In situations where high performance or reduced latency is a priority, configuring read preferences can come in handy.

6. **Configure Write Consistency**: Write concerns is another configuration option that controls how the write operations are done across replica sets in a cluster. To ensure data consistency across multiple data centers, MongoDB offers several write concerns settings

such as majority, which ensures that all nodes replicate an operation in the majority of nodes within the replica set to consider the write complete.

In summary, deploying and managing a global MongoDB cluster with multiple data centers and regions can bring many advantages to organizations, but it requires careful management and adherence to best practices. By carefully considering the above challenges and following the best practices, organizations can ensure that their global MongoDB clusters are reliable and operate optimally.

6.10   How do you troubleshoot and resolve performance issues related to the MongoDB oplog size and replication lag in a replica set?

The oplog in MongoDB is a capped collection that stores all the changes that are made to the database. It is an essential component of MongoDB replication since it allows secondary nodes to replicate changes made to the primary node. However, if the oplog size is not configured properly, it can lead to replication lag and performance issues. Here are some troubleshooting steps and solutions to resolve performance issues related to the MongoDB oplog size and replication lag in a replica set:

1. Monitor the replication lag: The replication lag is the time it takes for a secondary node to catch up with the primary. You can use the 'rs.status()' command to check the current status of replication and the replication lag. If the replication lag is increasing over time, it is an indication that the oplog size may be too small.

2. Check the oplog size: The default size of the oplog in MongoDB is around 5

3. Check the oplog utilization: The oplog should never be 100

4. Check for long-running operations: Long-running operations on the primary node can cause the oplog to fill up quickly, leading to

replication lag. You can use the 'rs.printReplicationInfo()' command to check for the longest-running operation. Once you identify the operation, you can use the 'db.currentOp()' command to get more details and take corrective action.

5. Optimize queries: Poorly optimized queries can lead to excessive use of system resources, including CPU and memory, which can lead to replication lag. You can use the 'db.currentOp()' command to identify the queries that are taking up the most resources and optimize them.

6. Add more secondary nodes: If all other options have failed, adding more secondary nodes to the replica set can help spread the load and reduce replication lag.

In summary, to troubleshoot and resolve performance issues related to the MongoDB oplog size and replication lag in a replica set, you need to monitor replication lag, check the oplog size and utilization, identify long-running operations, optimize queries, and add more secondary nodes if necessary.

6.11 Explain the role of MongoDB's logical sessions in coordinating distributed transactions and managing session-level data consistency.

MongoDB's logical sessions provide a way to group related operations together and coordinate distributed transactions across different nodes in a cluster. In addition to this, they also facilitate session-level data consistency by ensuring that data read within a session is consistent with data written within that session.

Logical sessions in MongoDB are created when a client connects to the database and can be associated with a particular client or application. Once a session is created, it can be used to group related operations together, even if those operations occur on different nodes in a distributed system.

When a session begins, MongoDB generates a unique session ID that is associated with the client or application. This session ID is included with all subsequent operations performed within that session, allowing MongoDB to group them together and treat them as a logical transaction.

For example, consider a scenario where a client needs to perform several operations that modify data across multiple collections in a distributed system:

```
// Start a new logical session
session = client.startSession();

// Start a transaction within the session
session.startTransaction();

// Perform some operations within the transaction
const result1 = await db.collection('collection1').updateOne({ ... }).session(
    session);
const result2 = await db.collection('collection2').updateMany({ ... }).session
    (session);
const result3 = await db.collection('collection3').deleteMany({ ... }).session
    (session);

// Commit the transaction
session.commitTransaction();
```

In this example, the client starts a new logical session, begins a transaction within that session, and performs several operations on different collections. The 'session' parameter is passed to each operation, allowing MongoDB to associate them with the same logical session. Finally, the client commits the transaction, causing all of the changes to be persisted together as a single unit of work.

If any operation within the transaction fails, the entire transaction is rolled back, ensuring that data consistency is maintained across collections within the session. Additionally, because the session ID is included with each operation, MongoDB can ensure that all reads performed within the session are consistent with writes that occurred within that session.

In summary, logical sessions in MongoDB provide a powerful mechanism for coordinating distributed transactions and ensuring session-level data consistency. By grouping related operations together under a single session ID, MongoDB can guarantee that all modifications to the data occur atomically and are consistent within the session, even across multiple nodes in a distributed system.

6.12   Describe strategies for handling schema evolution and data versioning in a MongoDB deployment.

Schema evolution is the process of changing the structure of the database schema, while data versioning is the process of keeping a version history of data changes over time. In MongoDB, strategies for handling schema evolution and data versioning can be grouped into three primary categories:

1. Manual Versioning: This approach involves manually tracking changes to the schema and data, including version numbers and any necessary migration scripts. While manual versioning offers the most control and flexibility, it can be error-prone and time-consuming.

2. Automatic Versioning: This approach involves using tools and frameworks that automate schema and data migration, such as the official MongoDB tool 'mongodump' and 'mongorestore'. Additionally, MongoDB provides native support for schema versioning using its $setOnInsert and $set operators, allowing you to set default values for fields that aren't present in existing documents.

3. Hybrid Versioning: This approach combines manual and automatic versioning by leveraging frameworks like 'Mongoose' or 'Spring Data MongoDB' that automate schema and data migrations while retaining the flexibility to customize the migration process.

Here are some specific strategies for handling schema evolution and data versioning in a MongoDB deployment:

1. Use Version Control: Using a version control system like 'git' to manage the source code and schema of your application can help you track changes to your schema over time. Additionally, committing a change to your schema to your source control system can trigger automated deployment tools to deploy the change to the production database.

2. Utilize Schema Validation: Schema validation allows you to define custom validation rules that apply when inserting or updating documents in a collection. By validating documents against a defined schema, you can ensure they match the expected structure and

values, preventing data integrity issues.

3. Design for Future Changes: Anticipating future schema or data changes and designing your database and application to support those changes can save time and reduce friction when changes occur. For example, using arrays instead of fields for a property with a variable number of values can make it easier to add or remove values in the future.

4. Test Changes in Staging Environment: Before deploying changes to production, test schema and data changes in a staging environment that mimics the production environment. This ensures that any migration scripts you've created work as expected and prevents unintended consequences.

5. Leverage MongoDB Atlas: MongoDB Atlas is a fully managed cloud database service that provides a variety of features for managing schema and data changes, including automated backups, point-in-time recovery, and change streams for tracking changes to the database in real-time. Leveraging these features can help you manage schema and data changes more easily and reliably.

Overall, choosing the right strategy for managing schema evolution and data versioning in MongoDB depends on the specific needs of your application and organization. Combining multiple approaches, like using version control and schema validation, can help ensure your database schema and data are flexible, reliable, and easy to manage over time.

6.13 What are the potential performance implications of using large ObjectId values as shard keys in a MongoDB sharded cluster?

In MongoDB, a shard key determines how data is distributed across shards in a sharded cluster. Choosing an appropriate shard key is a critical factor for achieving good performance in a sharded environment.

ObjectId is a 12-byte unique identifier generated by MongoDB for every document inserted into a collection. It consists of a 4-byte timestamp, a 3-byte machine identifier, a 2-byte process id, and a 3-byte counter. ObjectId is commonly used as the '_id' field of a document, which is also the default shard key in MongoDB.

Using large ObjectId values as shard keys can have several performance implications in a MongoDB sharded cluster.

Firstly, MongoDB uses range-based partitioning to split data across shards based on the values of the shard key. When ObjectId is used as the shard key, the values of the shard key are in the form of ObjectId, which are essentially timestamps. This means that queries that filter on a timestamp range could result in a large number of chunks being scanned in multiple shards, even if the actual data size is relatively small. This is because the timestamp values are evenly distributed across the entire range of 12-byte ObjectId, so the chunks will also be evenly distributed. As a result, queries that span a large timestamp range may perform poorly due to the increased network traffic and I/O required to read data from multiple shards.

Secondly, using large ObjectId values as shard keys can lead to hot shards. Hot shards are shards that receive a disproportionate amount of read or write traffic compared to other shards in the cluster. In the case of ObjectId as the shard key, the 4-byte timestamp in the ObjectId is updated every second automatically. This means that if documents are inserted at a high rate, the chunk that contains the latest timestamp values could become overloaded with writes, leading to hot shards. The problem becomes worse when reading data because queries are mostly interested in more recent data, which is stored on the hot shards. This can result in increased latencies and reduced overall throughput.

Lastly, using large ObjectId values as shard keys can result in uneven data distribution across shards. If ObjectId is used as the shard key, and document ids are generated in a monotonically increasing fashion, then most new documents will be inserted into the chunk with the latest timestamp value. This chunk will grow faster than other chunks and may lead to a situation where some chunks have significantly more data than others. This can lead to an uneven data distribution across shards, which can result in unbalanced utilization of cluster resources and reduced performance.

In summary, using large ObjectId values as shard keys in a MongoDB sharded cluster can result in performance implications such as range queries may involve multiple shards, hot shards, and uneven data distribution across shards. It is important to carefully choose an appropriate shard key based on the access patterns of your data to avoid these performance issues.

6.14   Discuss the best practices for monitoring and alerting in a large-scale MongoDB deployment to ensure proactive issue resolution and minimal downtime.

Effective monitoring and alerting are crucial for maintaining the high availability and optimal performance of large-scale MongoDB deployments. Here are some best practices for monitoring and alerting in a large-scale MongoDB deployment:

1. Set up monitoring tools: Several monitoring tools are available for MongoDB, including MongoDB Cloud Manager, Datadog, and New Relic. These tools allow you to monitor the performance of your MongoDB deployment, including CPU usage, memory usage, I/O operations, network traffic, and so on. Set up these tools to receive alerts when certain metrics exceed predefined thresholds.

2. Use monitoring agents: Monitoring agents can provide detailed information about the state of the MongoDB deployment. For example, MongoDB provides a monitoring agent named mongodump, which provides real-time statistics on various aspects of the deployment, including locks, connections, index usage, and more.

3. Create custom alerts: Generic alerts may not cover all the possible scenarios that could cause issues in large-scale MongoDB deployments. To ensure comprehensive coverage, create custom alerts that cater to your specific environment. For example, you may want to set up alerts for specific queries that take longer than expected to execute.

4. Monitor for replication lag: Replication lag is a common issue in MongoDB deployments. It occurs when secondary nodes in a replica set fall behind the primary node. To avoid this issue, set up monitoring tools to alert you whenever replication lag exceeds a certain threshold.

5. Monitor shard balances: Large-scale MongoDB deployments typically use sharding to distribute data across multiple servers. If one shard becomes too overloaded, it can lead to performance issues. Set up monitoring tools to monitor the balance of data across your shards and receive alerts whenever an imbalance occurs.

6. Monitor backups: Regular backups are essential to ensure that you can recover from any data loss or corruption. However, regular backups alone may not be enough – you need to ensure that the backups are actually usable in the event of a failure. Set up monitoring tools to verify the integrity of backups and receive alerts whenever a backup fails.

7. Set up multiple alert channels: Ensure that alerts are sent to multiple channels, such as email, chat, and SMS, to ensure that you receive notifications even if one channel is down.

8. Regularly review and update alerts: MongoDB deployments are dynamic, and changes to the environment can cause alerts to become outdated or irrelevant. Regularly review and update alerts to ensure that you are notified only when necessary.

In summary, monitoring and alerting are critical for maintaining the optimal performance and availability of large-scale MongoDB deployments. By following these best practices, you can proactively identify and resolve issues, ensuring minimal downtime and maximum uptime.

6.15 Explain the differences between various backup methods in MongoDB, such as filesystem snapshots, mongodump, and MongoDB Ops Manager or Atlas backup, and the trade-offs associated with each approach.

MongoDB provides multiple backup options. The options provide varying trade-offs in terms of backup speed, backup size, and restore capabilities. Here are the major backup options in MongoDB:

1. File System Snapshots:

File System Snapshots are a backup option that leverages snapshots taken at the operating system level. This option involves taking point-in-time snapshots of the underlying file system where the database data files reside.

Advantages:

- Fast and incremental, only changes since the last backup are captured.

- No impact on the application, performance during the backup process.

Disadvantages:

- Since file system snapshot backups are at the file system level, there are some additional implementation steps to be taken.

- Requires dedicated backup hardware and software, which is not cheap.

2. Mongodump:

Mongodump is a command line backup utility that creates a binary export of the data stored in a MongoDB instance. It generates a consistent backup of MongoDB databases and can run in a standalone mode or with Automation Agent.

Advantages:

- Saves individual collections for a partial backup.

- Backup to remote locations.

Disadvantages:

- Can be resource intensive for large-scale data as the command runs on a single node.

- Slower compared to file system snapshots and cloud-based backup options.

3. MongoDB Ops Manager:

MongoDB Ops Manager is a cloud service provided by MongoDB that provides automation and management tools. The service provides an easily configurable backup system.

Advantages:

- Automated backup scheduling and retention periods.

- Backup status notifications and user-based access control.

Disadvantages:

- Reliance on an external service provider with additional costs.

- Only on-premise support with limited cloud scenario.

4. MongoDB Atlas backup:

MongoDB Atlas Backup is a cloud-based backup service offered by MongoDB Atlas. Atlas backups continuously back up the data and can run across multi-regions. It's a fully automated cloud service offering that provides point-in-time recovery for replica sets and sharded clusters.

Advantages:

- Fully automated, no requirement for user intervention.

- Point-in-time restorations across multiple regions.

- Built-in compression and de-duplication capabilities.

Disadvantages:

- Added costs on top of basic MongoDB Atlas costs.

- Point-in-time recovery in minutes to hours based on data size and internet connectivity.

In conclusion, selecting the right backup solution depends on the specific use-cases of the company. Larger enterprise organizations may favor MongoDB Atlas Backup for its easy-to-use, cloud-based solution with a short recovery window. Meanwhile, smaller organizations may prefer the easier setup and management of MongoDB Ops Manager, while tech-oriented solutions opt for File System Snapshots to fit their more customized services.

6.16   How do you configure and use MongoDB's audit logging functionality to track and analyze database activity for security and compliance purposes?

MongoDB's audit logging functionality allows users to track database activity for security and compliance purposes. This functionality enables administrators to review and analyze the actions performed on each MongoDB instance. Let's discuss configuring and using MongoDB's audit logging functionality to track and analyze database activity for security and compliance purposes.

Enabling the Audit Log

To enable the audit log, you need to add some configuration settings to the MongoDB configuration file. The audit log output can be sent to either a file or a syslog server.

For a file:

```
auditLog:
  destination: file
  path: /var/log/mongodb-audit.log
  format: JSON
```

For a syslog server:

```
auditLog:
  destination: syslog
```

The 'destination' parameter specifies where the audit log output will
be sent, while the 'path' parameter specifies the file path of the output
file.

Audit Log Format

MongoDB's audit log can be configured to output in either BSON or
JSON format. The audit log can be customized by specifying one or
more of the available components:

- **authentication** - Logs authentication events such as login and logout
attempts.

- **connection** - Logs client connections and disconnections.

- **command** - Logs database commands executed by clients.

- **all** - Includes all available components.

Examples

Enable the Audit Log

To enable the audit log, add the following configuration settings to
the MongoDB configuration file:

```
auditLog:
  destination: file    # Output to file
  path: /var/log/mongodb-audit.log # Output file path
  format: JSON          # Output format as JSON
  filter:
    readWrite: true     # Log read and write operations
    users: ["jsmith"]  # Log operations performed by user "jsmith" only
```

This configuration enables the audit log and sets the output to a file
in JSON format. Also, it filters the audit log to only include read and
write operations and only those performed by the user "jsmith".

View the Audit Log

To view the audit log, you can either use a tool like MongoDB Compass or a command-line utility such as 'cat' or 'tail'.

```
cat /var/log/mongodb-audit.log | grep 'command.*users'
```

This command prints all commands related to user management, such
as create/update/delete user operations.

Analyze the Audit Log

The audit log can be used to identify unauthorized access attempts or suspicious activity. For example, if you notice several failed login attempts by a specific user, it may indicate a brute-force attack. Furthermore, the audit log can help ensure that the database is meeting regulatory compliance requirements by tracking database activity.

In conclusion, audit logging is one of the most critical aspects of any security strategy, and MongoDB provides a powerful, configurable tool out-of-the-box. By enabling the audit log, configuring it to output in the desired format and components, you can efficiently track and analyze database activity for security and compliance purposes.

6.17 Describe the process of setting up and managing client-side field-level encryption in MongoDB for data privacy and security.

Client-side field-level encryption in MongoDB enables you to secure sensitive data by encrypting specific fields of a document before it is sent to the MongoDB server. This means that even if the database is compromised, the data will be unreadable since the keys to decrypt the data are held outside of the database. In this response, we will describe the process of setting up and managing client-side field-level encryption in MongoDB.

Setting up Client-Side Field-Level Encryption

Step 1: Generate a Master Key

The first step to enable client-side field-level encryption is to generate a master key. This key will be used to create data keys, which will be used to encrypt and decrypt the data. The master key should be kept secret and secure since it is needed to access the encrypted data.

```
openssl rand -base64 96 > localhost.pem
chmod 400 localhost.pem
```

Step 2: Configure MongoDB

Once the master key has been generated, the next step is to configure MongoDB to use client-side field-level encryption. This involves
adding a JSON schema file to the MongoDB configuration, which
specifies which fields should be encrypted and how they should be
encrypted.

```
{
  "validator": {
    "$jsonSchema": {
      "bsonType": "object",
      "properties": {
        "ssn": {
          "encrypt": {
            "keyId": [
              {
                "$binary": {
                  "base64": "i0vK8WycTjuTLaT+B2NsdGXALvPhxmr1Z6Ufrj+jQds=",
                  "subType": "04"
                }
              }
            ],
            "bsonType": "string",
            "algorithm": "AEAD_AES_256_CBC_HMAC_SHA_512-Deterministic"
          }
        },
        "dob": {
          "encrypt": {
            "keyId": [
              {
                "$binary": {
                  "base64": "VYRcEu+UxVbN6WCfUd09Jiw+/+v/9XAOJ/cfOyHJjKs=",
                  "subType": "04"
                }
              }
            ],
            "bsonType": "date",
            "algorithm": "AEAD_AES_256_CBC_HMAC_SHA_512-Deterministic"
          }
        }
      }
    }
  }
}
```

Step 3: Create Data Keys

The next step is to create data keys, which will be used to encrypt
and decrypt the data. These data keys are specific to each field that
is being encrypted and are created using the master key that was
generated in step 1.

```
db.createCollection("temp",{
  "validator": {
    "$jsonSchema": {
      "bsonType": "object",
```

```
    "properties": {},
    "encryptedFields" : {
      ssn : {
        "keyId" : [
          { "$binary" : {
              "base64" : "<base64-encoded-key>",
              "subType" : "04"
          }}
        ],
        "encryptedAlgorithm" : "AEAD_AES_256_CBC_HMAC_SHA_512-Deterministic"
      }
    }
  }
 }
});
```

Step 4: Insert Encrypted Data

Now that the master key has been generated, MongoDB has been
configured to use client-side field-level encryption, and the necessary
data keys have been created, it is time to insert encrypted data into
the database.

```
db.temp.insert({
  ssn: "012-34-5678",
  dob: ISODate("1990-01-01T00:00:00Z")
})
```

Managing Client-Side Field-Level Encryption

Once you have set up client-side field-level encryption, you must manage it to ensure data remains secure.

Rotating Master Keys

Over time, it may become necessary to rotate the master key. This
can be done by generating a new master key and re-encrypting the
data using the new key. The process involves decrypting the data
with the old key and re-encrypting it with the new key.

Rotating Data Keys

Rotating data keys involves generating new data keys and re-encrypting
the data using the new keys. This may be necessary if a data key has
been compromised or if it has been used for too long.

Managing Key Access

Access to the master key and the data keys must be managed carefully to ensure data remains secure. Access to the master key should be restricted to only those who need it, and data keys should be generated and managed by trusted processes.

Conclusion

If implemented properly, client-side field-level encryption can be a powerful tool to secure sensitive data in MongoDB. It requires careful planning and management, but the end result is enhanced data privacy and security.

6.18   Discuss the potential challenges and best practices for scaling MongoDB's full-text search capabilities to handle large volumes of data and high query loads.

MongoDB provides full-text search capabilities through its text index. To handle large volumes of data and high query loads with full-text search in MongoDb, several challenges have to be considered.

The following are some of the potential challenges and best practices for scaling MongoDB's full-text search capabilities:

1. Data Sharding

In MongoDB, data sharding refers to the process of partitioning data across multiple servers. Since full-text search can become computationally intensive, sharding the data can distribute the query and indexing load across multiple servers.

For example, suppose a user has a database containing articles written in multiple languages, and the user wants to search for articles in a specific language. One way to achieve this is to shard the data based on language, such that articles of the same language are stored and indexed on the same server. By distributing the search load among different language-based shards, the user can reduce the response time of search queries.

2. Index Optimization

MongoDB's full-text search capabilities allow users to create and configure text indexes that optimize search capabilities. Some best practices for optimizing text indexes include:

- **Choosing the Right Analyzer**: MongoDB supports several text analyzers that handle language-specific complexities, such as stemming and stop words. It's important to choose the right analyzer based on the type of data and language of the text.

- **Indexing Only Required Fields**: To minimize the index size and query time, users should only index fields that are required for their search queries.

- **Optimizing Index Storage**: MongoDB provides different storage engines that handle data differently. For example, WiredTiger provides compression and data deduplication capabilities that can reduce index size and improve search performance.

- **Adjusting Index Weights**: MongoDB allows users to assign weights to indexed fields based on their relevance to the search queries. Assigning the right weight can improve search accuracy.

3. Query Optimization

To efficiently handle high query loads, users should optimize search queries. This can be achieved by using some best practices such as:

- **Using Text Search Expressions**: MongoDB provides powerful text search expressions that allow users to fine-tune search queries. Expressions such as *regexandtext* allow users to perform complex pattern matching and term frequency analysis, respectively.

- **Caching Results**: To avoid redundant search queries, users can cache the search results on the application side. This reduces the query load on the database.

- **Using Pagination**: To handle large search result sets, users can use pagination to limit the number of results returned per query.

4. Hardware Considerations

Hardware considerations are also crucial when it comes to scaling up MongoDB's full-text search capabilities. Some best practices include:

- **Using SSD Drives**: Full-text search can be disk-intensive, and using Solid State Drives (SSDs) can significantly improve search performance.

- **Increasing Memory**: MongoDB's search performance improves with more memory. Users should consider increasing the memory available to their MongoDB server to improve search performance.

In conclusion, scaling up MongoDB's full-text search capabilities requires considering and implementing several best practices. Data sharding, index optimization, query optimization, and hardware considerations are important factors that users should consider when optimizing their full-text search environment.

6.19   How do you handle backup and restoration of a MongoDB sharded cluster with complex data distribution and zone sharding configurations?

Backing up and restoring a sharded MongoDB cluster can be a complex and time-consuming task, particularly when dealing with a cluster with complex data distribution and zone sharding configurations. In general, there are several steps that need to be taken in order to ensure that the backup and restoration processes are successful.

1. Determine the data distribution and zone sharding configuration of the cluster: Before beginning the backup and restoration process, it is important to understand how the data is distributed across the sharded cluster and how the cluster is configured for zone sharding. This information will help determine the best approach for backing up and restoring the cluster.

2. Set up a backup environment: In order to perform a backup, a separate environment should be set up that is separate from the production environment. This can be accomplished by setting up a

separate deployment of MongoDB or by using a cloud service provider
that provides backup and restore capabilities.

3. Take a backup of the primary shards: Once the backup environment has been set up, the first step is to create a backup of the
primary shards in the cluster. This can be accomplished using the
mongodump utility or by creating a snapshot of the disk where the
primary shards are stored.

4. Take a backup of the config server: In addition to backing up the
primary shards, it is also important to create a backup of the config
server. This can be accomplished using the same methods as for the
primary shards.

5. Restore the config server: When restoring a sharded cluster, it is
necessary to restore the config server first. This can be accomplished
using the mongorestore utility or by restoring a snapshot of the disk
where the config server is stored.

6. Restore the primary shards: After the config server has been restored, it is necessary to restore the primary shards. This can also be
accomplished using the mongorestore utility or by restoring a snapshot of the disk where the primary shards are stored.

7. Rebalance the cluster: Once the primary shards have been restored, it may be necessary to rebalance the cluster in order to ensure that the data is evenly distributed across the shards. This can
be accomplished using the shardCollection command with the option
to force a shard key range split.

To illustrate this process, below is an example of how to backup
and restore a sharded MongoDB cluster using the mongodump and
mongorestore utilities.

1. Determine the data distribution and zone sharding configuration
of the cluster

```
mongo
use config
db.chunks.find()
db.collections.find()
```

This will output the current distribution of chunks across shards and
the collections and their associated shard keys. You will need this

information to backup and restore the data properly.

2. Set up a backup environment

Using the cloud provider or vendor specific tools to create a replica set or a dedicated backup environment with a copy of the primary shards and the config server.

3. Take a backup of the primary shards

```
mongodump --host [host] --port [port] --out [backup directory]
```

This will create a backup of the primary shards in the directory specified.

4. Take a backup of the config server

```
mongodump --host [config server host] --port [config server port] --out [
    backup directory]
```

This will create a backup of the config server in the directory specified.

5. Restore the config server

```
mongorestore --host [config server host] --port [config server port] [backup
    folder]
```

This will restore the config server from the backup folder.

6. Restore the primary shards

```
mongorestore --host [host] --port [port] [backup folder]
```

This will restore the primary shards from the backup folder.

7. Rebalance the cluster

```
use admin
sh.enableSharding(databaseName)
sh.shardCollection(collectionName, shardKey)
sh.splitAt(databasename.collectionName, splitValue)
```

This will split and distribute collections based on the shard key configuration.

In summary, handling backup and restoration of a MongoDB sharded cluster requires careful planning and execution. By following the steps outlined above, administrators can ensure that their sharded cluster is properly backed up and can be fully restored in the event of any data loss or disaster.

6.20 Discuss the architectural considerations and best practices for integrating MongoDB with other data storage and processing systems, such as relational databases, data warehouses, and data lakes.

When integrating MongoDB with other data storage and processing systems, such as relational databases, data warehouses, and data lakes, it is important to take into account architectural considerations and best practices to ensure a smooth and efficient integration. Below are some guidelines:

1. Understand the use case and data requirements: Before integrating MongoDB with other systems, it is important to understand the use case and data requirements. This includes understanding the types of data that need to be integrated, the frequency of updates, and the performance requirements.

2. Choose the right integration approach: There are different approaches to integrating MongoDB with other systems, such as using ETL (extract, transform, load) tools, custom scripts or connectors, or APIs. The choice of approach depends on factors such as the complexity of the integration, the volume of data, and the frequency of updates.

3. Normalize the data: When integrating MongoDB with relational databases or data warehouses, it is important to normalize the data to ensure consistency and avoid data duplication. This involves breaking down the data into smaller, standardized tables with unique keys, and establishing relationships between them.

4. Use appropriate data models: MongoDB's flexible schema allows for a wide range of data models. When integrating with other systems, it is important to choose the data models that best fit the use case and data requirements. This includes deciding on the level of denormalization, choosing appropriate indexes, and using appropriate data types.

5. Optimize performance: Performance is critical when integrating MongoDB with other systems, especially when dealing with large volumes of data. This includes choosing appropriate hardware and network configurations, optimizing queries, and using appropriate indexing strategies.

6. Use appropriate security measures: When integrating MongoDB with other systems, it is important to ensure that appropriate security measures are in place to protect the data. This includes using encryption, authentication, and access controls.

Examples of integrating MongoDB with other data storage and processing systems are as follows:

1. Integration with a relational database: Suppose we have a MongoDB database that contains customer information, and we need to integrate it with a relational database that contains order information. We can use an ETL tool such as Talend to extract the data from MongoDB and transform it into a relational format before loading it into the relational database. We can then use a JOIN query to combine the customer and order information when querying the data.

2. Integration with a data warehouse: Suppose we want to integrate a MongoDB database containing sales data with a data warehouse to perform business intelligence analysis. We can use a custom script to extract the data from MongoDB, transform it into a normalized format, and load it into the data warehouse. We can then use SQL queries to perform analysis on the data.

3. Integration with a data lake: Suppose we have a MongoDB database containing sensor data from IoT devices, and we want to integrate it with a data lake to perform real-time analytics. We can use the MongoDB Connector for Apache Spark to stream the data from MongoDB into Apache Spark, where we can perform real-time analysis

using Spark's distributed computing capabilities. We can also store the data in a data lake such as Amazon S3 for long-term storage and batch processing.